GARDEN
in the
EAST

The Spiritual Life
of the Body

ANGELA DOLL CARLSON

ANCIENT FAITH PUBLISHING
CHESTERTON, INDIANA

Published by:
   Ancient Faith Publishing
   A Division of Ancient Faith Ministries
   P.O. Box 748
   Chesterton, IN 46304

Unless otherwise noted, Scripture quotations are taken from the New King James Version, © 1979, 1980, 1982 by Thomas Nelson, Inc. Used by permission.

ISBN: 978-1-944967-03-1

Printed in the United States of America

The author and publisher gratefully acknowledge permission to reprint the following materials:

"So it is with the Spirit" in Luci Shaw's *Scape*
Eugene, Oregon: Cascade Books 2013
© 2013 Luci Shaw
Used by permission of Wipf and Stock Publishers.
www.wipfandstock.com

Joyce Sutphen, "Living in the Body" from *Straight Out of View*,
Joyce Sutphen
Holy Cow! Press, Duluth, Minnesota, 2001
Reprinted with permission

For my mother—
who has planted, nurtured, and watered
this garden of me without fail

CONTENTS

How secretly the bones move

under the skin

and the veins thread their way

through their forests, the trees

of bones, the mosses of cells,

the muscle vines.

How privately the ears

tune themselves to music heard

only in the echoing cave of the head.

And the tongue in its grotto tests

the bitterness of unripe fruit, and wine,

the mouthfeel of honey in the comb.

How cunningly our shadows

follow us as we walk.

And our breath, how it moves in

and out without great thought.

Even rain, which needs no summons from us

but flows, a gift from heaven,

as the grasses rise greenly, shivering.

Just so, beauty besieges us

unannounced, invading us, saving our souls.

So it is with the Spirit.

LUCI SHAW, "SO IT IS WITH THE SPIRIT"

THE BODY IS A GARDEN

The LORD God planted a garden eastward in Eden, and there He put the man whom He had formed. And out of the ground the LORD God made every tree grow that is pleasant to the sight and good for food. The tree of life was also in the midst of the garden, and the tree of the knowledge of good and evil. (Gen. 2:8–9)

There is an oak tree in the middle of a field on our property in Tennessee. It rises from a stand of long prairie grasses native to that region. At one time, that field was a pasture for horses. Perhaps there was once a barn there. We find old rusty horseshoes in the dirt from time to time. We find nails, bits of board or leather from the straps of saddles. Wildflowers now populate the place around that tree—spring cress, coneflower, southern blazing star. In the spring, the tree is surrounded by the field-dwelling plants.

We cut a small trail through the field, to the tree, around the trunk where once a swing hung. Now, only an aging rope hangs there; the swing's seat lies buried below the grass, a vague remembrance of the past. When the cold weather comes, the tree drops its leaves, the grass browns, and we cut down the large stand of the prairie to make room for new life that comes again when Earth moves back into the springtime cycle of this region.

The tree is accessible in these cold weather months. I can put my hands on the cold bark and imagine what kind of life it might have led. I can look up to the bare branches and count them now. The tree, even while dormant like this, offers some clarity that was obscured in the distracting bloom of the warm weather. The tree becomes a story—the roots, the trunk, the branches. And the field that surrounds this tree becomes the book that holds all the stories of the inhabitants of this place—the soil, the plants, the wildlife, the weather. The field is a garden here, tended by an unseen gardener.

When I let the land bring itself back to life season after season, I discover something new with each passing moment. When the sun is hot and the summer is sweltering, I walk on the path through the rising prairie grasses, purple cone-flower, and brilliant flight of butterflies to stand at the foot of the oak in that field. I think to myself—I am like this tree, with roots deep and branches reaching out, and I am this place, this wide world garden. And this body that carries me into the field, into the kitchen, into the grocery store is a garden—living, breathing, seasonal, blossoming. This body is a garden.

❈❈❈❈❈❈❈❈❈

THE FIRST GARDEN I REMEMBER was that of my grandmother. She and my grandfather lived in the house next door to ours. The tiny brick ranch-style house was a stark contrast to our white clapboard farmhouse. Their house was modern and well kept. Ours was old and worn down and lived in. Compared to many of the houses on Briarcliff Avenue in the Shiloh neighborhood of Dayton, Ohio, the ranch-style house was relatively new. When my grandparents built it, they already owned the farmhouse we now lived in. They already had the plot of land the garden crops occupied and the greenhouse that sat just in front of that land. They built the new house and rented the old one to us.

My grandmother tended that garden with great care, and in later years she kept bees as well. We'd wander through the rows of corns and beans and rhubarb, touching the leaves with our small hands, feeling the dirt that crept into our shoes. I remember this garden in patches of memory, and it has remained in me as a kind of longing and not much more. I didn't inherit my grandmother's talent with plants and growing things. I'm a terrible gardener.

I am the great plant destroyer, killer of all things green and leafy. Though I am "she of the brown thumb," I am still drawn to living things, especially to plants and gardens. I paste pictures of them on my walls in the winter. In Chicago, the winter can be brutal. When I'm living in the city, I'm often absent even small hints of the promise of spring. Instead of grassy patches that begin to green around me as the seasons change, I see well-traveled hard-cracked concrete, sometimes covered in pollution-colored snow. Slush and mud and leftover road salt mark the alleys and roads as I drive my kids to school. When the ice and snow melt at last, making puddles and revealing winter's buried city litter— this is how I know that spring is coming.

Still, I try to garden. I feel a spark when I see pictures of flourishing gardens. I want to grow something beautiful, something that develops and reaches out leafy fingers toward the sun. The stark reality about gardening is much more brutal than the lovely pictures I see in the seed catalogues and gardening magazines. The seeds grow, tender and tentative, and then yes, they flower, but they also wither and die—and that's a hard pill to swallow. In my case, they wither and die quickly, usually from lack of water or attention. It is a matter of paying attention, I think. That's where I fall down.

When I was young (or maybe just when I was younger), I didn't think about aging or death. I thought only about the now, the here, the present tense. My skin was mostly clear; my body was adequate for my needs. I did not necessarily *feel* young, but I was young. Things were relatively new and worked the way they ought to work. That's a blessing I took for granted. The constant refrain of being young is to take our youth for granted. When we are young we spend our youth, like money we got in a birthday card from an elderly relative.

As we age, we try to store that youth, now pennies on the dollar, now locked in a storehouse inside of us. It feels more precious to me the older I become. Each new season, each new decade, holds some gathered wisdom. It transcends the merely physical. This set of hands builds things that bridge me to the world—in my parenting, my partnering, my prayer life. These things weave together as the garden weaves together with the air and the rain and the wildlife—as one part influences all the other parts of the ecosystem.

Over time, I've come to see that the way I care for and nurture my body has implications in all areas of my development—physical, emotional, and even spiritual. This realization ignited in me a new interest in reconciling the needs of the physical body with the needs of the spiritual life resident in that body. I am, once again, standing in the field or at the foot of that oak tree in Tennessee, hands on the bark of the trunk, feeling the texture and imagining there must be more happening there under the surface; life teems everywhere around me. This is not machinery. I am not machinery.

It's a popular notion, this idea that the body is a machine or a race car, whether fine-tuned or failing. But my body reveals to me a much different story. I am not metal-made but organic and alive. If I am a spirit in a vessel, then that vessel is most decidedly more clay than contraption, more soil than soldered, more plant than plastic. This body is a garden.

The body I am tending is a living and organic revelation of the unseen spirit inside. We are sacraments of the One who made us, "beautifully and wonderfully made," as the psalmist would say. I am given charge of this garden from season to season, from birth to death. So, what if I tend to the body the way an attentive gardener would his garden? What then? What is the watering? Where is the history buried here beneath the oak? How do I help to bring about the blooming of springtime flowers even as I embrace the stretch marks and surgery scars in the skin that covers my miraculous muscles?

I admit my struggle in overcoming my terrible history in gardening—whether it refers to my literal care of plants or the essential care of the body. There are pitfalls to this caretaking in either respect—a risk of becoming too focused on physicality, or conversely too negligent. There is a risk that I might either lose sight of the big picture or become obsessed with it. There is drought and there is flood. The goal has to include balance.

In an ever-tilting world, perhaps this is where I find the real challenge. It may not be that I'm not paying attention.

It may be that I am not keeping the balance that nature demonstrates to me season after season. I begin then with this basic truth, a thought that guides me throughout this journey into wellness, and wholeness, and these adventures in spiritual and physical horticulture. This body is a garden. It is organic and alive, intricately woven together by the hands of the One who made me, and it needs my care. The body is a garden.

CHAPTER ONE

THE HEALING

On Persistence and Perception

To say that I am made in the image of God is to say that love is the reason for my existence, for God is love. Love is my true identity. Selflessness is my true self. Love is my true character. Love is my name.
　　　　　　　—Thomas Merton, *New Seeds of Contemplation*

I wore yoga pants all day today. I admit that I put them on because I was feeling a little puffy, a little bloated perhaps. After returning from a week away from home, I recognized that my eating and exercise habits while on vacation were lacking. It's possible those habits had been lacking, in fact, even before the vacation came. Stress does that to me. Stress does that to a lot of people. I know I'm in good company. After stepping from the shower that first day back from vacation, I had a quick look in the mirror, and the first thought that sprang to my head was bitter and condescending. "Oh God, I'm getting so fat. I hate my thighs."

My daughter is a tender seventeen-year-old willow tree of a girl. She is strong and capable, an activist, a powerful beauty. At no time in my parenting of her would it ever have occurred to me to comment negatively on her body. At each juncture of development, I went out of my way to instruct her to love her body, to care well for it. I gave her affirmations. I gave her what I hope was a good foundation. It occurred to me, after voicing those criticisms from my quick post-shower glimpse in the mirror, that if I ever talked to my daughter the way I talk to my own body, it would be downright abusive. Why the disparity?

Once I saw a movie in which a man was hitting a child. When one character in the movie attempted to stop the abuse, the man looked up from his terrible work and said, "He's mine! I can do with him what I want!" Here I am, offering up verbal barbs to my own body day after day in the same way. It's mine! I can do with it what I want!

My body and I have lived together over forty-seven years now. There has never been a time in our temporal lives when we have not been intertwined. We are inseparable, living out our days in mutual habitation. We have everything in common except for the abuse I heap upon it. My body is good to me; it gives every single day. My body processes air without complaint, as though it were no trouble at all. It houses the systems of life, pumping blood, moving muscles, and obeying impulses from my sometimes foggy brain or my often misguided will—and then I step from the shower and say awful things to it.

I wore yoga pants all day today because my jeans are too tight, my ample muffin top spilling over the edges, a constant reminder of poor choices in either fuel or fashion. I pine for a return to the fashion styles of the 1940s. I consider Betty Grable wearing a bathing suit that stopped where my muffin top would naturally ebb. I consider the classy style of Katherine Hepburn rolling up the sleeves of her starched white dress shirt tucked carefully into those high-waisted dress pants as she gives Spencer Tracy a piece of her mind. I wonder if she ever said haughty things to her body. I wonder if Betty Grable hated her thighs.

I saw a quote recently that struck a chord. It read, "Mother Teresa didn't walk around complaining about her thighs. She had stuff to do." Life's too short to complain about our thighs, after all. But I do it, and I'm pretty sure every woman I know, and some of the men as well, do it even though we all have stuff to do.

It's easy to fall into the habit of complaint. It's easiest to do it in the privacy of my home, in the intimate moments when I'm alone, in the moments just after I step from the shower after a long week away, after an eight-hour drive with only fast food to quell the hunger that creeps in. As I drive and eat, I imagine the perceived poisons leaching into my cellulite, even though in more sane moments I know it's not literally poison, and there's nothing unnatural or bad about my cellulite. But I worry because here, in the middle-age part of my life, every small choice matters. I can no longer rely on a fast teenage metabolism. I can no longer rely on the willowy build I see in my teenage daughter. I can no longer rely on my body to make up the difference, and so when I step out of the shower and see the havoc I've wreaked, of course it's easy to blame the messenger.

I wore yoga pants all day today because of the comfort but also because of the shame and the built-up resentment and anger I hold. I am sorry, Body. I am sorry for it. I am sorry for the harsh words and the tight, constricted clothing meant to contain the damage I've done. I am sorry, Body, for the bad meals and the shortcuts and then the blame placed on you. I am sorry for the years of talking trash about you to myself, to other people, to the doctor and the personal trainer.

I wore yoga pants all day, and I discovered you again, every curve, every bulge, every cell. I held you again, wrapping my arms around you when I would begin to forget that we're in this together. I placed my hands on my thighs, on my rear, on my belly. I said, "I love you, lots and lots, Body," and I cried a little each time, afraid I would not believe it's really true—but it is true. So I wore yoga pants all day and I let my body breathe easy, and I breathed easy, and I ate spinach and broccoli instead of French fries just this once at least, and we both agreed it was a good choice.

There are three possible stances one can take towards the body. One is the worship of the body, when the body is idolized and all interest and attention is turned towards it. In patristic terminology this is called self-love. Another attitude is the rejection of the body, which is a central view of all dualistic and idealistic systems. The third stance is the Eucharistic approach, according to which the body is viewed as God's gift and is offered to Him together with the soul. Orthodox theology has the third view.

—Metropolitan Hierotheos of Nafpaktos

THE FIRST YEAR I PLANTED A GARDEN, I put in three small rows of lettuce. The seeds for your basic bib lettuce are tiny, and I didn't trust the smallness of them, the depth of the planting, the spacing, and my own lack of skill and knowledge. I put them in at the prescribed time, according to the directions on the back of the seed packet mixed with advice from the books available to me.

And then, as with all things in life, I waited. I planted and I waited. Much to my surprise and delight, they did sprout and grow, and what survived neighborhood rabbits, the cold snaps, the beating sun, and the forgotten watering days resulted in a very fine salad I placed on the table, with great pomp and ceremony, before my hungry children. One salad. It was delicious but mostly underappreciated and, upon further consideration, short-lived.

I was not thinking about anything at the planting apart

from sprouting seeds. I had not considered that perhaps staggering the planting of something as delicate as lettuce would extend the fruits (or rather lettuces) of my labors for the entire growing season, or at least for a few more meals than just that one. My small labors felt inconsequential at that moment. The long-term goal felt impossible.

❈❈❈❈❈❈❈

THE PICTURES I KEEP taped to my wall for inspiration show flourishing, fecund gardens. They are well established—years or even decades in the making. It's likely that professionals tend these gardens, looking to the care of them regularly with a dedicated team. But it's also possible it's simply someone who decided long ago that an overflowing and gorgeous bounty of flowers, fruits, and edible plants of all sorts was something they wanted to see outside their window every day. I'd like to have that view. I'm just not sure I have the patience or persistence for it.

I keep this quote by St. Isaac the Syrian taped to my wall as well: "A small but always persistent discipline is a great force; for a soft drop falling persistently, hollows out hard rock." When I first became Orthodox, I had some trouble starting up a prayer practice according to the Tradition. I tried to jump into it with both feet, following what would amount to a monastic-level prayer practice, praying many times a day the full complement of prayers that were suggested in the tiny blue prayer book I'd been given. I was exhausted quickly and interrupted every few seconds by my children's needs. They were young, and I was a little bit desperate for peace. I wanted it *right now* because, as I mentioned, my children were young and I was worn out. I keep that quote on my wall to remind me about my prayer practice, but it works for other good habits I am trying to foster as well—exercise, eating, keeping in touch with other humans—things I want to be doing but seem not to do as well as I hope.

When I consider how many things I yearn for *right now*, I think first of the condition of my physical body. It makes sense that I'd go there first, my body being so fully present to me in my every waking moment. Even when I was in my early twenties, I had more criticism than praise for my level of fitness, my weight, or my flexibility. I talked ugly to my thighs and my face.

It was a conditioned response, I suppose. We are taught in strange but certain terms to be uncomfortable in our own skin. We are surrounded by messages and images that support the thinking that we ought to be yearning for another face, another body, another level of physical prowess. Not only are we encouraged to want it; we are expected to embody it *right now*. This is why the "get fit quick" scams rake in so many followers. This is why I am tempted by them every single time I see one, and why I sometimes give in.

I want to make a change, but I don't want to wait for the

results. I want to start a program that will shift my body, burn the fat I don't want, "detox" the liver or pancreas or kidneys, and restore me to some former health or a perfect physique, even if that former health or perfect physique never really existed—and it doesn't exist. The whole thing is a ruse, a lie made up to sell more products, to hollow us out and make us believe we are in need of something that can be supplied easily with creams or clothing, programs or cosmetic surgery.

We are in need. This much is true. The emptiness is real, and the garden must be planted. But the marketplace offers to replace the long-growing heirloom seeds our deep garden deserves with artificial flowers made of silk and silicone, plastic plants with stiff-leafed promises.

I live in the shadow version of myself when I buy into the flawed quick-fix, miracle-cure thinking—and then even if I receive the promised benefits of these changes, I often find that I'm still not satisfied. It's a hard lesson to learn that sometimes after sowing seeds, and watering, and waiting I'm still not happy, not content, not fulfilled. I end up with one small salad on the plate, and it is mostly unappreciated. I look around the neighborhood and start to compare my neighbor's flourishing garden to my own floundering, first-year attempt. That is the affliction I carry through it all—comparison mixed with impatience is deadly.

I want to believe a miracle pill exists. I want some easy,

quick fix, but I cannot simply change one aspect of my life in order to see real change. This wild place needs more than a cosmetic clipping. Wild places need careful tending. I will have to dig deep to free the soil and the roots. I have to change the way I think about the body, the way I think about health and wellness, the way I think about what (or who) is beautiful and worthwhile and valuable. I have to start to hammer away at the old messages, and that needs to happen before I even begin to make changes to what I eat or how I move. This is groundwork. But it starts even deeper than that, even before I leave the metaphorical potting shed and move into active tilling of that soil.

I consider for a moment what I might say to this body/child that I love but with whom I am not pleased at that moment. Should I withhold love until the body changes or does something that shifts that perception? Why would I even consider saying these ugly things to this body? To withhold love and care based upon those criteria would be an action that shows an obvious lack of compassion, an obvious lack of the deep and abiding love that is required in order to flourish and grow. Why the disconnect? Habit, conditioning, a lack of awareness, or maybe I just have never been given permission to love this garden, to heal it and to see it as beautiful already, worthy and able.

In those moments before I have seen anything change, before the tilling, before the planting, before I've had a chance to even see first signs of new life in this garden, it's difficult to remember that shifts in body composition or health take time to unfold. I am planting a garden that will sustain me, and I ought to be thinking in those terms. I am not growing a single salad for a single meal. I am planting seeds that will rise from the seedling into winding vines. Some will flower and then wilt. Some will produce fruit, some only leaves that will become compost. Each part of me works in harmony then with the other parts, the eyes and ears, the brain and feet, the hands and heart.

Choosing a quick fix won't work for the long term, because if I begin to look to the root of things, to the hard-packed clay soil, I will see that change has to come from a deeper place. The healing this garden needs usually isn't about simply what the scale reads or how the pants fit. It's not only about dissatisfaction with the belly or the thighs. The healing involves all the parts of the process—the daily living out of faith, eating, movement, as well as the emotional, spiritual, and mental wellness.

As I do the hard work of cultivating the spiritual and emotional view of my body, as I make these small but persistent changes in my diet, calorie intake, hydration level, or exercise level, I am only working on the surface of good health. I am planting a temporary garden, one that will only last a season rather than a lifetime. Certainly, the popular, glossy images all around me, held up as an example, don't help this process much. I try to remind myself that the pictures of people in fitness magazines and fashion billboards do not tell a true and complete story. I only see what the industry wants to show.

The real and true story of health and wellness, as it pertains to *my* life and *this* garden, is the one I write with the One who made me. This is the tilling of the soil of the garden, and it heals us. It knits together the divide that opened up between who we are now and who we think we ought to be or want to become. This is a place of promise. It's hopeful and messy. This tilling begins with the recognition that I am valuable, body and soul, and worthy of care and cultivation. The healing begins here, when I say to myself as I look in the mirror, "This body is good," even when I want with all my heart to criticize, to nitpick, to tear down or walk away.

It's emotional and spiritual strength training. Every commitment to change my perception and bring it into alignment with the Creator's good design builds over time and lays a firm foundation for change, for blooming and growth. The healing of the garden starts here—first perception and then persistence. Preparing the soil starts before my hands even touch the earth, and it continues well into planting season.

CHAPTER TWO

THE DIVIDING LINE

On Balance

*Then God said, "Let Us make man in Our image, accord-
ing to Our likeness; let them have dominion over the fish of
the sea, over the birds of the air, and over the cattle, over
all the earth and over every creeping thing that creeps on
the earth." (Gen. 1:26)*

The body is mystery. It begins in the dark, tucked
into that warm, innermost place—building
in the quiet confines of the womb. It begins with the cells
dividing, the flesh forming, the organs growing. The body
is mystery and wonder. The first heart sounds, the first kick,
the first waving of arms and legs floating in that safe place.

I consider the holy conversation in Genesis—about making mankind in the image of the Creator. We are a sort of
self-portrait of the artist; the process of art-making hidden
inside. In that art-making there is this conversation happening with the Divine, directing the body, infusing the
spirit, the quickening, the transition to the outside when the

time comes. It is a true fact that at this writing, the medical community is not one hundred percent sure of what triggers the birth process. They do know, hormonally, perhaps chemically, the chain of events that occurs. They know how the process unfolds as labor begins, obviously, but the spark that kicks off the whole thing is something the medical community cannot pin down. Like a seed in the soil, it is a combination of things, lining up as some kind of ancient innate prescription that brings the new person, at last, into the bright sun above ground.

When my daughter was born, she noticed her arms first— her arms and her hands. Her newborn body lay on the bed next to mine. She was entering this new world, breathing air, no longer surrounded by the warmth of amniotic fluid. She lay on her back adjusting her eyes to the light, waving her arms because gravity caused them to splay out in that way. Inside my belly she was subject to the laws of that environment, but out here in the wide world, she had to adapt.

What a shock it must be to enter a new realm with a new set of laws that determines our relationship to the natural world. Out here, the air is cold, the light is harsh, the sound is overwhelming. This is why, during labor, when she reached the end of the birth canal and her head was crowning, the nurses dimmed the lights in the room. We made sure there were warm towels ready. We made the place ready for our girl, to soften the transition to come. Even so, after the initial shock of entering this new world, she cried, testing her lungs for the first time.

As she lay on her back on the warm towel that helped to dry her, she flailed her arms to the sides, up and down, extending them with her tiny hands in fists. It was a new experience. Inside the womb she would kick and punch from time to time. She would glide her arm or foot too near to my ribs, and I would adjust my position to catch my breath. Out here she was liberated into the air. All movement was available.

In infancy the body is so basic, so overtly mechanically challenged against the elements, it's tempting to resort to thinking about the machinery of us. I watched her discover the world those first few hours of life. I saw that she noticed her arms first. I was there when, lying on her back after just arriving, she waved her arms to the sides and caught sight of that arm. She turned her head slightly to one side so she had a better view and watched the waggling of her arm, her hand still in a fist. She watched the arm as it bounced up and down, and then she unclenched that fist. She pursed her lips and waggled that arm again. She tightened her fist again and played this, perhaps her first game, for several minutes.

She was a miracle unfolding before me. She was all mystery to me and to herself. This moment was mystical, and it was sacramental. I drank it in, her delight and mine. Hers was a sacramental exploration of the mechanics of her body in the world, in the air, in the odd gravity of this new life.

Mine was an exploration of new motherhood, unwrapping the mystery of this small person. I kept thinking how miraculous she was and how terrifying it was that someone felt I was trustworthy enough to take charge of this new human in our midst. We both had to discover the operating procedures for this new endeavor. Sometimes it was by reaching out into the air, waggling the arm. Sometimes it was by seeking advice from other people, books, or instinct. Sometimes it was trial and error. It was always engaging the mystery of that process.

The body is mystery, and from birth it's our task to discover it, to explore our understanding of it—the way we move, the way we feel, where we can reach out into the air with long limbs and open hands. And the body is functional, too, abiding by a set of standards and measures that lead, ultimately, to its best use and purpose. Gravity, weather, weight, heredity, history—these things all figure into physical health. The mystery and the sacrament, the form and the function, they work together within this intricate and beautiful design.

❋❋❋❋❋❋❋❋❋

Awakening and surrender: they frame each day and each life; between them the journey where anything can happen, the beauty and the frailty.
—John O'Donahue

THERE IS A SLIM SPACE, for me, between utility and appreciation. Whether in life choices or road trips, I often choose
the practical route because it gets me wherever I need to go
more quickly and efficiently. I just want to get there. There
are times when I will take the opportunity to enjoy the scenic
route. It helps if I am not the one driving. As for gardening,
the sensory experience is in the wandering; the appreciation
is for the finished product, or at least the already fruitful
version of that product. Gardens of my family members or
friends, or the Botanic Garden in Chicago, or Cheekwood
Botanical Garden near our house in Nashville—all of these
have afforded the sensory experience of beauty without my
having to do any of the work. When I am not the one doing
the heavy lifting, I am free to stand in awe of that creation.

Bringing that beauty home and creating a version of
this in my own back yard holds another, more tactile, gift.
This is where I see that I am lacking. A moment of realization comes after I arrive home from purchasing the flat of
annuals from the grocery store parking lot one fine spring
morning. I remember then that I do not own a spade or a
gardening shovel. I look at the flat of flowers waiting for the
transfer into a larger setting—clay pots or tilled rows in my
yard. They do not care.

I stare at the purple pansies and yellow buttercups for a
long time, trying to imagine them in that bare space along
the fence. Rather than heading out for a suitable tool, I grab

the heavy-duty shovel my husband has in the garage, the one that still carries traces of dried cement, and I set to hacking up the plot of yard that I think is, more or less, a kind of rectangle. It takes me most of the day. The flowers are wilting in the heat. I am wilting too.

Once I finish that task, I dig holes for the purple and yellow blooms. I try to position them in their current plastic housing around the space I have prepared, to test for depth. I think I remember that I ought to dig out a hole deep enough for the entire root ball, and then I dig just a bit more, for good measure.

Once they are in the ground, the newly fashioned, makeshift flowerbed dwarfs the tiny plants. One flat was not nearly enough for the space. It is too late to replace the grass I've taken up. Though it is late in the day, I head to the local garden center. I pick out a cheap brown plastic border for the area. I pile a few more flats on the cart, thinking maybe they'd spread out over time. I pick up a spade, designed for the gardening job, some gardening gloves, and a bag of soil I hope is the right sort for the bed I'm building.

After a few days of buying, digging, planting, trial and error, fingers crossed and nails broken, the flowerbed is finished. It lasts a couple of weeks in all its glory before a large section dies. The area those flowers took up got little to no sun because of the angle of the yard and a neighbor's tree. A few weeks after that another round of plant deaths peppers the flowerbed. I pick off the dead buds and see that the soil is overly wet still, the drainage of that part is poor, the soil underneath is mostly clay-like and doesn't support the roots. I hadn't thought of it before. It's something I discover later, when I've had the chance to think it through and ask some advice from people who know.

The decision to put in a flowerbed was not planned, not well thought out, not considered with a bigger picture in mind. It was an impulse. I wanted that beautiful view, that garden I drive past on my way to the grocery store or the one that resides in the yard of my neighbor. I want it now, and so I set out to make it so. I am living there in that slim space between beauty and frailty, appreciation and utility. Everything seems possible in those slim spaces.

It's exciting at first, then sobering in practice. The reality of the situation is that I was in too much of a hurry to occupy that beautiful place I wanted to create. I was not willing to find the beauty in the planning, in the research, in the digging, the bordering, the planting and watering. Following a plan and the rules for approaching a big project, like this one, has its gift too.

It is in this step that I find I am most inclined to rush in without thinking, and this ultimately leaves me wanting—with big empty muddy holes staring back at me instead of immense beds of flowering plants. I rush into the mystery of that beauty. I delve into it without considering the finer points, the sacramental elements that make up the vision before me. And so the end product is never what I hoped it would be. Trial and error, live and learn.

In gardening, we're meant to take into account all the physical elements of the space we're working with, giving them equal weight and attention. In setting up the flower bed, I might have spent time planning the space, marking it, watching the sun for a day or two, checking the soil, and then choosing which plants were best suited for the space. Where my health is concerned, the mechanics of the human body need this same consideration, this same reverence and respect. Some aspects of the garden are mystery, a matter of discovery, given to time and patience and waiting; and some aspects require research, forethought, consideration, and planning.

When my health fails or my waist expands, I blame my body. I jump to this—*my body is bad.* But when my flowerbed failed, I did not blame the flowerbed. I did not blame the flowers I chose (though that might have been an easy target). They were not "bad" pansies. They were simply not given the proper environment.

I seem to work most frequently through trial and error like this, trying and failing and trying and failing until finally a pattern emerges, a theme, a habit, a routine. I create a disconnect between the mystery and the sacrament, forgetting the relationship between hand and air, child and parent, plant and water; but they are related. All the parts work together.

I divide my body itself too—when I talk about having a bad back or bum knees, I separate that part from the whole. When magazine covers shout from their wire racks as I enter the line in the grocery store—"Get thinner thighs!" "Lose that muffin top!"—in that moment I place my hands on my tender tummy, my well-crested muffin top, and wonder how I might do more crunches, eat this magical fruit to shrink that part or stay a little longer on the treadmill to work this off. The goal becomes pinpoint, narrow, honed into one offending part.

This is a dividing line I draw, sometimes without even thinking, where the body and spirit are concerned, but this divide doesn't truly exist. I am not simply a series of parts operating in the open air. It does me no good to factor out one piece, one element, one plant, from another. This is the set of plants I am working with, the soil in which I'm planted, the sunlight I am offered, the season I am entering. The more I know about how this system of me functions and flowers, the better I can choose the course of care for the entire garden. This is what balance promises. This is what choosing to take a long-term vision affords.

IN ALL THESE THINGS, physical and spiritual, I want to move toward balance, even if it means trial and error is my entry point. I have to start someplace. Balance figures into all the aspects of maintaining this garden, whether it is our approach to prayer, diet, or workout. I have to take into account all the elements in that garden. So unless I'm working with an injury that requires special attention to one muscle over another, improving an inherent weakness or recovery time, I'm always going to want to treat the body as fully integrated—muscles and sinew inserted at joints and folded into one another. No one part works alone. I'm reminded that though St. Paul was speaking metaphorically in drawing an analogy between the work of the physical body and the Body or followers of Christ, the analogy is strong because the comparison is true:

And the eye cannot say to the hand, "I have no need of you"; nor again the head to the feet, "I have no need of you." No, much rather, those members of the body which seem to be weaker are necessary. And those members of the body which we think to be less honorable, on these we bestow greater honor; and our unpresentable parts have greater modesty, but our presentable parts have no need. But God composed the body, having given greater honor to that part which lacks it, that there should be no schism in the body, but that the members should have the same care for one another. And if one member suffers, all the

members suffer with it; or if one member is honored, all the
members rejoice with it. (1 Cor. 12:21–26)

WHEN I'M TEMPTED TO MAKE an invisible dividing line
between good and bad parts, I hope I remember the dividing line is not real. We are not separate components of soul
and body but integrated and whole. I hope instead I take
the time to plan well, to discover the path of the sun, the
seasonal shifts, the planting zones. I hope I'll aim for middle ground when I'm inclined to want to move into criticism rather than cultivation, that I'll choose the best possible position for setting realistic, attainable, and holistic
goals where health is concerned. When I adopt this posture, embracing the mystery and the mechanics, taking into
account the whole of the garden—spirit, mind, and body—I
find I begin to form better relationships, more positive
attitudes, and a gracious acceptance of myself where I am at
this moment, rather than reaching for the person I wish I
were, or the body I wish I had.

The body is mystery, and the body is sacrament, form and
function. I look to the place where that imaginary dividing
line seemed to reside. I used to think I had to walk as on
a tightrope between the body I have and the body I think I
ought to have. High on that wire, I would run from one pole
to another, or find myself clinging to the wire when I was
near to falling, hands chafing from the cold metal on my

fingers. My arms would splay out, as my baby daughter's did as she discovered the world, in an effort to balance myself, to right myself, to feel my boundaries, to find my balance.

But I see now that line is erased, invisible, and the ground is firm under my feet. With feet firm on the ground, we find that the balance we seek, while we still struggle for it, takes on a different feel. We are safe here, walking in the garden—spirit, mind, and body together. I am not at odds with gravity, with the wind blowing, with the current season. I am working in conjunction with the natural process of this life unfolding.

I will have to remind myself of that often as I tend the garden. I will have to remind myself that I am safe here, that this is my plot of land, my flowerbed, my stand of trees, my wandering vines. And this frames the structure of my garden—my days and my life and my journey, the beauty, the frailty, the possibility. Anything can happen.

CHAPTER THREE

FALLING WELL

On Shortcomings

Therefore strengthen the hands which hang down, and the feeble knees, and make straight paths for your feet, so that what is lame may not be dislocated, but rather be healed. (Heb. 12:12–13)

It was my first time skiing, and I was doing really well. I need to say that I was, in fact, doing really well because what happened on that last run of the day was a textbook error for a first-time skier. It's a little embarrassing—I fell, and I fell badly. I had heard before I started skiing that day that there is a good way and a bad way to fall. The good way to fall is to land on your backside. Essentially, if you think you're going to fall, then the preferable course of action is to sit down, so to speak. I did not do that. I fell badly. My only excuse is that after skiing all day I was tired, and this run was harder than the ones earlier in the day. I was exhausted and tense. I fell ski over ski over ski, tumbling down the slope until I came to a stop in a heap of snow on the edge of the ski run. I fell badly because I did not take time to practice falling, and so I forgot in the moment how to fall well.

I felt the pop in my knee as I went down and then the pain. I cussed a little, and then I tried to stand, but by then the knee was already swelling. It had been a long time since an injury brought tears to my eyes as this one did. My tears on the slope were a mixture of anger at myself, embarrassment in the moment, and pain from the fall. I sat on that snow-covered hill watching people glide down around me, and I cried as my husband unstrapped the skis from my feet. A passerby called the ski patrol, and a few minutes later, I went down the rest of the mountain on a stretcher pulled by a twenty-something ski-patrol kid. He showed great skill as he zigzagged speedily down the mountain while the sun dimmed and the sky grew dark.

I confess that the ride down the mountain on the stretcher was the most fun I had all day. I think I actually giggled as we swished along. I realize now that it was fun because I wasn't worried about falling. I spent most of that day focusing on just staying upright. I was not gliding, as the confident skiers around me seemed to be. I was busy worrying about falling, but on the ride down the mountain on that stretcher, I was able to trust the skill of the ski-patrol kid. On the stretcher I was thinking only about the wind in my face and the crunch of the packed snow under the sled while I watched the sun set over the mountain, making long shadows of beautiful trees, casting rays of red and gold between the green of the pines. I did not care in the least about the pain in my knee or the pitying looks on the faces of the other skiers.

One might think it would be easy to fall well, but it just isn't. When someone tells me to sit down if I think I'm falling, it might sound like solid advice from the safety of the bunny slope; but on the other runs, when I'm out on the mountain, tearing down a snow-covered hill toward the advancing stand of trees, it turns out the idea of sitting down is far from the front of my brain. What pushed its way to the front of my thoughts in that moment was sheer terror, along with the phrase "I am going to die on this mountain." Generally, I'm not productively problem-solving when I'm falling. I'm just trying to stay alive here.

✿✿✿✿✿✿✿✿✿✿✿

FEAR HAS AN ACTUAL, physical effect on the body. The body stiffens up, movement becomes awkward, breathing is shallow, and thinking is fuzzy. It feels impossible to relax, to exhibit some control, to just live in the moment. When I'm afraid and I fall, I get hurt despite my best efforts to right myself. The fear might even be worse than the actual fall. I miss too much on each run down the slope just being afraid of the impact. What's worse is that sometimes after a fall, I'm less inclined to want to start again.

This cycle happens for me on a spiritual or emotional level, too. I make an attempt to walk (or ski) the straight and narrow, and then I hit a metaphorical tree, or I just fall badly before hitting the tree. The snow is icier than I expect, I'm more tired than I know, the hill is steep, the wind is cold, the skis are slick, the day is long. The hard part is remembering in the middle of that run how to fall well—and that takes time and practice, being willing to fall over and over if necessary. It's a risk. Just getting up and starting again is a risk.

I never climbed back on a pair of skis after that fall. I tell people it was because our family kept growing, our finances kept shrinking, we never found the time. In reality, though, if I'd wanted to go skiing again, I'd have found a way to do it despite all those limitations. I fell badly and I was injured and I was afraid to try again. I figured there were at least three hundred other things I'd rather do than try to pick up skiing again. I let fear inform the way I would go forward. I cut my losses, and maybe that's okay for the short run, but in the long run what does it benefit me to shy away from learning new things or trying again?

<hr />

What is this mystery in me? How am I to understand this divine blending of body and soul?

—St. John Climacus

STRESSORS THAT ARE REAL in garden tending—lack of water, poor soil quality, rough weather, invading insects, poor attention to the relationship between the types of plant life—push into the day-to-day. They suck the air from the room; they crowd an already crowded brain and body. I don't always see the connection between external stresses, my internal fears, and illness or injury. Despite the intrinsic blending of body and soul, I am still a citizen of the culture in many ways. And it means I will always be encouraged to operate with a degree of duality—the physical here, the spiritual there.

If I return to the metaphor of seeing this body as a garden rather than a machine, I start to understand, as most gardeners understand, that we are more than the sum of our plants. Deeply rooted fears, falls taken long ago, become ongoing buried stressors that have a profound effect on the health of this body. And because all the elements of this garden exist together, this becomes a systemic issue. All the elements of health—weather and soil conditions, plant choices, seasons, wildlife—either support and nurture or can cause destruction to the flourishing of that garden. I feel that pounding heart, that reluctance to try again, and I bury it deeper, pressing it down into the dark soil until, over time, it becomes clay and chokes the roots of anything else I hope to plant.

So falling well isn't only about practice as a protection

from a potential injury. The stored-up fears I keep hidden like heavy rocks in my pockets from previous falls need addressing as well. I know that running into a tree will hurt me, certainly, but sometimes even the fear of running into the tree has the potential to injure. Tensed muscles and foggy thinking will throw me every single time; it makes me question my training, my practice, my commitment. In that moment I don't want to fall; I just want to quit before I even begin.

Where is the middle ground there? Why do I keep planting things, keep carving out places to grow things? Why do I keep bringing houseplants home when old ones die? Every time I replace the sad sagging orchids on my counter, I wonder where I went wrong. I wonder why I don't just invest in some cheap silk plants and call it a day. I persevere, standing up over and over again as often as I can, because I want to be better at the caretaking. One day it may work. One day I may realize the tiny herb garden I keep on my windowsill is thriving and has been thriving for far longer than I remember.

I set the goal and work toward it, and yet often, too often, I feel I fall short. And yet, I'm human. How can I help but fall short? I know somehow deep inside that embracing the struggle is the thing, that identifying the fear and engaging it is vital. It is how I begin to understand this blending of soul and body. If I learn nothing else from reading the

Desert Fathers, it is this basic instruction—to embrace the struggle. It is nurturing this garden, even when the stressors creep up—and they do, of course they do. If I stop trying because of previous failures, I'll never get the flourishing garden. I tell myself in those times that maybe I don't care for gardening, that I have no interest in it, but I don't really mean it. Fear makes us lie to ourselves. It makes us unwilling to get up and try again.

Fear can be piercing and immediate, as when being chased by a bear or perhaps barreling down a mountainside with slick fiberglass boards strapped to one's feet and not nearly enough instruction for the task. The heart pounds, the adrenaline kicks in, the muscles tense, waiting for impact. But fear can also be resident in us. Stored from long-past experiences, stored in the brain and the heart, stored in the muscles that remember the fall and remember the injury. I can be nowhere near the mountain and still feel the fear gnawing in the pit of my stomach. I can still feel the heart pounding, though it's tempered by the safety of my armchair.

I may yet avoid the mountain, but knowing about that fear and admitting its influence is important. It keeps me in touch with the reality of my situation. It's humbling in that context and yet it's empowering as well, if I'm willing to embrace it. And I am willing to embrace it. I want the well-nurtured garden. I want to see the progress that comes with commitment and consistency.

I will fall down again in the soul and body tending. I'll forget the vegetable servings and optimal hydration guidelines. I eat too much candy in one sitting. I drink too much at the office party. I skip the workout. I take the escalator instead of the stairs. Sometimes it's defiance, sometimes it's forgetfulness, and sometimes it's caused by the fear of failing. If I let those small lapses define me, I am lost, and then I wonder, "Why bother?"

When I reach those places in the gardening, this is where I ought to remember to sit down, to fall well. I have to keep in mind that what I'm after is progress, not perfection—I won't get far if I set perfection as the benchmark. I will not start on the slope the first time and glide along like the seasoned skiers around me. I'm not a sporty savant. I have to learn to stand on the skis, I have to practice balance, I have to learn to turn when I start going toward that stand of pine trees. I need to learn how to stop and how to fall well, to just sit down once in a while when I feel out of control, and I need to practice those things too. For as long as I let fear of failure rule, or for as long as I believe I shouldn't fall, I'll never make it to middle ground—and that is where I most need to be.

It occurs to me now, years later, that the feeling I had on that stretcher as we barreled toward the warmth of the ski-patrol headquarters is perhaps the feeling that keeps people coming back to the ski slopes time after time. I glimpsed it there—as the wind rushed over my face and the confident ski-patrol kid glided easily down that last run of the day while I lay safely strapped into the sled. I imagine that with some practice and a little more courage, I might find that feeling of freedom on the slopes again, but this time I would also hope to gain the feelings of control and accomplishment in the process. I did not give myself permission to fail before I began, I did not practice falling, and so when I fell badly I let that be an ending.

I know now that the loss was not only physical, but also emotional. I wonder how I let that loss and fear bleed into other challenges and other opportunities over the years since I fell down on that slope. I want to do it better. I want to practice the falling, the getting up and brushing off the snow from my legs and arms. I don't want to dwell in the fear any longer. Sure, I am a terrible gardener, but I will keep trying—trial and error, as usual, and then trying again. It may not be pretty or graceful, but the gift is in the attempt. Shooting too far one direction or the other is of little consequence in the long run down the steep slope. It is the pursuit of middle ground that gets us to where we want to arrive, hopefully without torn ligaments to show for it.

CHAPTER FOUR

UNDER THE SKIN

On Beauty

Who is capable of gazing upon the Garden's splendor?
Seeing how glorious it is in all design, how harmonious in
*   all its proportions*
how spacious for those that dwell there, how radiant with
*   its abodes?*
                —St. Ephraim the Syrian, *Hymns on Paradise* 2:8

In my best moments, I am grateful to be walking around, upright and active. In those moments, I am not noticing the forward jut of my head, misaligned from age and bad postural habits built up over time. I am not worried about the creaking of my knees or my elbows. In my best moments, I am thinking about deep issues like world peace and schoolyard bullies and what's for dinner.

I sometimes stand with fists at my waist and elbows out, like Superman in a classic pose of power. They say (as the anonymous "they" are wont to say) that if I do this every day for only a few minutes, I'm bound to feel good about myself.

I stand in the Superman pose and throw my shoulders back, suck in my gut and lift up my chest. It does feel powerful. I can almost see the chiseled abs appearing. I can almost feel them all washboard at the belly. If only it were true. Instead of washboard abs I have quiet cushioning that wraps around my hips and haunches. It reaches around the whole of my waist, like a comforting hug from a well-meaning aunt. I did not ask for this thickening, but midlife granted it to me anyhow.

The cultural fix-it promise I always fall for is the one that comes late at night when I'm poking that paunch that spills out over the top of my pajama pants. The promise comes in a pill, or if I'm lucky a tasty citrus drink. Just add water. It burns fat. It blasts away the belly. It has my name written all over it. "Take it once a day," the promise coaxes, "and maybe do these seventeen exercises too." This promise has rosy lips, smiling and sultry. This promise costs only $39.95 for a three-month supply. This promise is sexy, and I am struggling to stay true to the quiet cushion of my hips and my belly that offers the comforting hug I did not ask for, the one that came with midlife, stretch marks and all.

This is a good body—strong, courageous, supple, and soft. It is the one and only body I have. I remind myself of this when I look in the mirror, when I hitch up my jeans along the leg and thigh, over the rounding of my belly and hips and bottom. "This is a good body," I say aloud as I stand in my Superman stance, but I do not always believe it. I am haunted by that late-night promise of a pill I can take to make it so.

The pill promise comes accompanied by a full-color photo of a young woman's torso—muscled and tanned. Her string bikini is a perfect shade of coral. Her hips are toned and her belly tight. I bargain with my psyche. "This is only temporary," I say. But instead of washboard abs I have a stitch in my back and crackling knees. My doctor tells me I should not worry about that crackling. So long as there is no pain it's natural, it's normal, it's within reason given my age. I'm not so old. I'm just barely middle-aged now.

Over time, gravity takes its toll, cartilage begins to wear away, so that walking up the steps with loads of laundry, my knees make it sound as though I'm carrying cellophane in my pockets. I remember cellophane—wrapping baskets of fruit, flowers, or nuts. My grandmother brought those baskets to the house when they arrived, gifts of friends or relatives. I remember the sound, the crackling, the static in my ears.

My grandmother's skin was flawless, her smile wide and breathy. She was always willowy in her build, even when she was old. The last time I saw her she might have weighed ninety pounds, lying in that hospital bed, dying from cancer. She was not wearing makeup. Her hair was a mess. She was concerned about that, but not about the cancer.

There is no good cure for aging. Ponce de Leon never

found that fountain of youth. In 1521, he was injured in Florida in a fight with Calusa warriors. They say he was shot by a poisoned arrow, probably in the thigh. He died in Cuba not long after. There is a beginning, and there is an end, but this is the middle. It is rough, but it is transitional. There is still much to discover in this body as a garden.

I'm reminded of a passage from a book I loved growing up, *The Secret Garden* by Frances Hodgson Burnett, in which budding gardener Mary Lennox and her friend Dickon discuss the finer points of the garden they've discovered:

> *"I wouldn't want to make it look like a gardener's garden, all clipped an' spick an' span, would you?" he said. "It's nicer like this with things runnin' wild, an' swingin' an' catchin' hold of each other."*
>
> *"Don't let us make it tidy," said Mary anxiously. "It wouldn't seem like a secret garden if it was tidy."*

Sometimes it seems that I woke up and found myself here all of a sudden, living this middle-aged version of myself. I catch sight of this body, this secret garden, in the mirror, and I am surprised. It is wild and untended but alive, so very alive. In *The Secret Garden,* Mary finds the key to this wild place buried, long forgotten. This realization, this discovery that I am so very alive, is the key, unearthed. The decision to love this one body I've been given, the decision to care for it well.

When I see myself in that mirror, I have in mind two

choices—look closer or look away. If I choose to look away, to leave the key buried, to leave the door locked, I am missing the beauty. I am disconnected from the whole of me. If I choose to look closer, I have to be careful about what I say; I know that what I say about my body goes right to my hips and right to my head. I have to rein in the resignation and keep from hammering away at my self-esteem, my motivation to care well, my inclination to give up, lock the door, and never look back. This body is a garden, and it is mine. I am responsible for its care. I am responsible for the words I use when I describe it, even to myself, even when I'm alone. Looking closer can be tricky, too.

Today, as I stand in my Superman pose, arms into fists dug into my widening waist, I am thinking about this wild and growing garden. This good body, this strong body, this one body I've been given, reflects back to me here, in this moment. This body I'm discovering is a little bit wild, like the secret garden Mary Lennox finds with the help of a cheeky robin.

You have it too, this wild, secret garden. The key is the thing. It's the starting place. We need that key, the one presumably dropped so long ago, planted there and then turned up with tilling or lawn care or time. We need that key, not a pill or a tasty citrus drink, not the belly blast or fat burner. We need that key to unlock the motivation, to offer the care we did not know we needed, the discovery of those places in us that have been forgotten, left untended too long. Dig for that key daily, scouring the ground for it. Search until you find it, and then be brave, pull back the ivy and unlock the door. There is still much to discover.

⁂

The only lasting beauty is the beauty of the heart.

—Rumi

ABOUT A HALF HOUR into putting some leafy red and gold blooming plants into a brand new, waist-high planter on my patio, I felt pretty good. *This will be my year,* I thought to myself. I sifted the cool soil through my fingers, digging out a deep hole in which to place the quivering plants. "Don't worry," I said to them, "it'll be okay." Though I was not fully convinced of this, I felt some renewed confidence nevertheless.

I thought I had it all under control as I finished filling the raised bed finally and grabbed two plants that remained on the red brick patio. These would find their new home on the deck above the garage. I would place these plants gently into those waiting clay pots. I would talk to them sweetly. I would assure them I could be trusted with their little lives and future blooms. I was having all kinds of amazing revelations from fingers digging into dirt and all that. I paid no attention to the soggy flip-flops on my feet, the tiredness in my arms, the heat of the day, and I missed a step going up.

Simple enough, but with no hands free to break my fall, it was my face that met the edge of the wooden steps.

I lay there only a moment before standing up. I was still processing what had happened when the blood began to pour from my face, dripping on the stairs in ripe, round dots. I ran inside, panicked and swearing. I grabbed a clean dish-towel and pressed it to my bleeding, throbbing face. My husband called out to ask if I was all right, to which I answered a loud and definite "no." He ran inside to survey the damage as I lay on the kitchen floor, pressing that towel to my nose. He asked to take a look, but I was afraid to release my grip— my eye hurt, my nose hurt, my hands hurt—but eventually, I relented. I kept my eyes closed tightly, as though that would allay the damage.

"How bad is it?" I asked, and when he hesitated, I withdrew the question. I pressed the towel back to my face and I thought about how good I had felt only a moment before, about those tender plants I'd carried, almost blooming already and in need of replanting. I tried to remember their name, finally finding it in my memory as I lay there bleeding on the kitchen floor. Salvia.

I chose the salvia because they're beautiful and hard to kill. They tolerate drought conditions and neglect, and they produce a stalk of tiny blue flowers which, they say, attract hummingbirds. I've never seen a hummingbird in Chicago, but I thought it was worth a try. I savored the irony in that moment that the name of the plant derives from the Latin *salvere,* "to feel well and healthy, to heal."

As I lay there bleeding, I worried that I'd broken my nose, I worried that I'd punctured my eye, I wondered about the lasting effects of my clumsiness on that familiar landscape of my face. I thanked God that I was not alone on the kitchen floor and that my husband was making the plan for our move from the floor to the emergency room. My two younger boys rushed in and sat near me after hearing the commotion, and when Dave told them I was hurt, they stroked my head and my hair. "Don't worry," they said, "it'll be okay." In those moments before the bleeding finally slowed enough for me to move, a thousand thoughts raced in my head about the body and the garden and the hidden dangers of gardening and flip-flops.

On the way to the ER, I joked that I'd gotten the idea I ought to title this book about gardening and the body "The Badass Gardener's Guide to Spirituality." I said I might put a picture of myself with my newly blackened eye, the gash across the bridge of my nose, and the thoroughly skinned knuckles on both hands. Behind me, I thought, we'd have a flourishing garden next to an old Army tank being used as a planter. I'd wear camouflage overalls and combat boots. I'd carry a rake and a hymnal. But really, I kept thinking about my face. What kind of damage had I done there? What would I see when I looked in the mirror?

The nurse asked what had happened, and I said, "Extreme gardening. It's all the rage." When she didn't respond, I copped to the more reasonable but terribly boring explanation, "I fell up the stairs of my deck carrying two plants. My face broke my fall." She nodded at this, took my vitals, and offered me an ice pack while I waited. I thought of the stitches that were sure to come, the black eye already developing, the bruised thigh and scraped knuckles, and of the salvia still sprawled out on the offending steps, scattered and spilling soil, withering in the heat of the lingering afternoon sun. Salvia, meaning "to heal."

I have my Grandma Doll's eyes, hooded and blue. The older I get, the more I see her in my face when I look in the mirror. The wrinkles that emerged sometime after my thirtieth birthday are around my eyes and my mouth at the edges. Laugh lines. I'm not unhappy with those.

My nose came from my mother's mother, proud and a little bumpy in the middle. I never cared for it. I thought it was far too big for my face, though I could point to it as some mild proof of my Cherokee relatives on my mom's side of the family. It was the bridge of this fine, proud, bumpy nose that broke my fall.

The doctor said the "fatty" area, where the bridge meets the forehead, took the brunt of the cut, and that is where he glued my face back together. The cut was jagged and red at the edges when he finished. I had two black eyes to boot.

I was a mess, and it took a long time to heal. I spent some time paying attention to my face, how it changed from day to day, how it felt when I caught a glimpse in the mirror. It's strange to say that I found beauty there, but I did. It's hard to explain.

The body is remarkable in its ability to heal, given time and care. In time, the black and blue receded from around my eyes, the nose skin knitted back together, reddened and faded, and finally became smooth again. I can still see the scar when the light is right. I run my finger over it sometimes, strangely proud of the nice job my skin has done in response to my clumsy footing while gardening.

The garden is remarkable too in its cycles of death and rebirth, injury and healing. Those salvia plants survived the fall on the steps. My husband planted them when we got home from the ER that day, and they bloomed more brightly in the following weeks than the other plants around them. I took a special interest in those plants, noticing them every day, holding no grudges about the fall. It's my own fault; I ought to have been paying better attention. I admit, though, I don't wear flip-flops while gardening anymore. Lesson learned.

<hr />

SOMETIMES WE DO NOT KNOW the beauty we possess until we fall. There is a tendency to want to see things only clean and blooming, but in the bleeding gash on my face I noticed the beauty of healing in the process. Being able to put aside the prescribed ideas about what is beautiful and what is not is a foundational part of becoming whole and healthy. We have to train ourselves to see the beautiful in the ordinary, in the injured, in the dying, as well as in the brilliant bloom of summer.

My eyes report, but it is my brain that assigns the merit of beauty—the curve of a lip, the clarity of skin, the leg length or arm reach, the color and texture and quality of everything I see. But no matter what my eyes report, there is beauty that lives under the skin, under the surface, under the standards set up for me by outside arbiters of what is good and true. Those arbiters are not always so reliable. They can be bought and sold. They can be marketed and manufactured. The real standards, the ones set forth by the One who made me, are solid, knitted into me at my beginning. This beauty is true and real, and it lives within the heart. It is my *heart* that must be trained to recognize this beauty.

The beautiful is identical with the good, for all things seek the beautiful and good at every opportunity, and there is no being which does not participate in them. They extend to all that is, being what is truly admirable, sought for, desired, pleasing, chosen and loved.
　　　　　　—St. Maximos the Confessor (*Philokalia* Vol. II)

IN THE ORTHODOX TRADITION, we look to those who have gone before us, their actions and their writings, for guidance. One such resource for this guidance comes from a large body of work called *The Philokalia*. The word means literally "the love of the beautiful." The *Philokalia* is a long work, spanning four thick volumes and sporting many authors throughout. It is a collection of words and ideas all centered on the pursuit of this task, to love the beautiful. It is not surprising to note that this love of the beautiful has nothing to do with hairstyles, fashion, or weight loss goals. All of the topics approached by the writers of the *Philokalia* focus instead on shifting our perspective away from the worldly and toward that of the Creator. The love of the beautiful becomes a deep endeavor, requiring effort and patience.

It's easy to see the secular notion of beauty. If I'm not discerning, I may believe that what is beautiful is whatever the latest marketing and advertising companies are pushing. I might begin to think that beauty depends on a dress size or a facial structure. I might get the wrong impression that beauty is some physical constant across all body types, skin colors, and histories—but it's not. I know somewhere deep inside of me that it's not this at all, and yet it is still difficult to move toward what is real. Beauty is, in its most simple and profound form, the reflection of God—and that is a far more compelling and lasting definition.

The pronouncement used in the creation story in Genesis,

once something is made, is that God saw that it was "good."
In the Hebrew this word is *tov*, meaning literally "pleasing
to the eye." I find that I resist calling the creation of me
"good." I tell myself it is humility, but this isn't humility.
It's a game I play with myself to keep expectations low or to
seek outside affirmation. There is a risk in moving toward
appreciation, toward gratitude, toward care and love of the
creation, toward calling it *tov*. I risk disappointment. I risk
being disenchanted. I risk rejection. What if I am wrong?

Leonardo da Vinci reportedly said that a work of art
is never finished, only abandoned—and this feels right.
Though I like to think this sense of "abandoning" a work is
less about leaving or giving up the work and more about letting the work leave us for a life of its own, as we do with our
children in parenting. When we do it well, or as close to well
as we can, at some point in the creation process we can pronounce it *tov*, and we let it go. We release that work into the
world, ready to live as something new. It is an act of trust.

When the artist creates a work and is finally able to step
back and pronounce it *tov* in the best sense of the word, in
the human understanding of the word, what the artist is saying in that moment is that the work reflects what she hoped
to bring forth, as well as it can within the scope of her skill
to bring it to life. What is before her is as close to what she
had hoped for or envisioned as she is able to come. This is *tov*
in the Creation sense of the word—a reflection of the One

who made it. In the case of God as Creator, that creation is, indeed, the vision put forth. But God arrives at *tov* without the hesitation and doubt we harbor as humans. He sees what is made as good from the start.

Seeing something as beautiful not because the culture deems it so but because we are able to see a reflection of the Creator in it should begin to shift our perceptions of ourselves. In order to see our bodies and, by extension, the whole of us as beautiful, truly beautiful, we must set aside our old perceptions of beauty in favor of a lasting and true standard. The standards that magazine articles and billboards offer are transient, dependent on an earthbound view. In order to know this, I must shift my perspective to the ethereal, to the eternal view of what is beautiful. This takes some work. The cultural deck is stacked against me. It takes daily reminders, daily reading, daily affirmation. In doing this, I am, in a sense, rewiring my thinking and my feeling.

I am like a piano in need of tuning. The strings are in place. The structure is good. If you have ever heard a piano tuner at work, you'll know that it takes a length of time striking the strings and listening, adjusting too high, too low, over and over. It is a precise and measured process. It sounds awful at first, and then when the string finds its tune, it is beautiful—true and smooth. The chords reverberate, humming together. The sounds suddenly seem to make sense; they are more than individual strings. The sound becomes

music, just as in a garden when the seeds become plants—
something new, alive and blooming. But how do we find this
tuning?

✸✸✸✸✸✸✸✸✸

> When God calls creation tov, this is not a moral, intel-
> lectual, or aesthetic evaluation. It is, rather, creative and
> consecratory "speech" by which God simultaneously brings
> Creation into existence and blesses it. That which is good
> and beautiful is blessed. That which is good and beautiful
> fits God's purpose in creating it. The creation is good and
> beautiful because it gloriously reflects God's own perfect
> being.
>
> —Vigen Guroian

THE FIRST TIME I HEARD ABOUT the Jesus Prayer was in a
poetry reading. The poet spoke about the prayer with such
depth and such passion that I was moved. The poet said
the prayer "tunes the heart to God." He said the prayer
"descends" into the *nous*, that part of us which sees—sometimes called the heart, sometimes called the intellect.

I imagine the nous here in my chest, wrapped in my ribcage. Sometimes I tap my fingers there on my sternum and
imagine the words of the prayer descending to that place—
Lord Jesus Christ, Son of God, have mercy on me, a sinner. So the tap-
ping there, on my sternum, reminds me to be present, to
be open, to be ready to hear and receive. The descent of the
words of the Jesus Prayer to that ready and willing nous is,

in large part, a pathway to peace for me. I fall into the prayer as often as I am able, sometimes without even thinking about it. It's become a habit because I spent time practicing the prayer as a response to stress—and I'm stressed all the time.

Saying the prayer becomes like drinking water in response to being thirsty. The trouble is that most of us deprive ourselves of this water for so long, we do not know that we are thirsty. We develop the dry mouth, the parched throat, the throbbing headache and accompanying stomachache, and we do not connect it with a need to become hydrated. Saying the Jesus Prayer in response to stress or harsh self-criticism is a way of hydrating, and in so doing, it tunes the heart to God. It puts us back into right relationship with the Creator. We get on the right wavelength to realign our perspective. Where the perception of beauty is concerned, I need this realignment.

The key to changing or realigning our understanding of beauty will always begin in the heart. The shift begins in the daily working out of our own perceptions of what is beautiful. When we tune the heart to God, we make a good start in doing this. If we are in tune with the Creator, then all of Creation takes on a new look. Even in the most difficult circumstances, being in tune with the One who made us gives us a depth of perception that is too often lost in the glossy pages of fashion magazines and the dishonest digital alterations of the bodies we see in our daily media. Reciting the

Jesus Prayer is not a miracle pill; it is simply a foundational element to that tuning. The strings are within us already. The structure is good. The Jesus Prayer is the thrumming on those strings, the sounds that reverberate through the whole of us, with time and with patience, and with practice.

Just as gardens take time and care, patience and persistence, the daily task of prayer is the path toward the eventual goal of praying without ceasing. If we think about the garden as a living and growing organism that is sometimes flourishing, sometimes fallow, the one constant is that the garden is always still the garden. Whether the leaves are brown or the grasses overgrown, it is still the garden. This daily work is a cultivation that takes place no matter the season. The real test of our progress will not be the condition of the garden but rather our ability, over time, to see the beauty inherent in it, regardless of its condition.

Apart from the One who made me, no one should love this garden more than I do. Love, in this usage, doesn't mean to elevate the body above the spirit or the mind, but rather to respect and honor that creation, to bring it back into alignment, into right relationship to the spirit and the mind. No one can compel me to love my body better, to respect it further. I set the standard for that love based on my history, and unfortunately, too often that standard is skewed and twisted. We realize after damages and injuries that come in the wake of misperceptions that the true standard ought to come from the Creator. It's a revelation to hear this truth—that we are created *tov*, that we are worthy of care, chosen and loved.

When I am tuned to the Creator, when I am in line with His idea of what is beautiful, I can see that beauty even in the wilted bloom, in the hard-frozen earth, in the rain-soaked pots, in the lightning-struck tree. When we are in tune to the One who made this garden, we can begin to see it through His eyes. We know already that He has pronounced it good, beautiful, pleasing to the eye—*tov*. And when we accept that He is right in His pronouncement, everything changes. Beauty may well be in the eye of the beholder, but this tuning the heart to God gives us the ability to see ourselves through the eyes of the Creator. We become the beholder. We recognize the beauty of the garden—and that is really something.

CHAPTER FIVE

SEASONS

On Aging

Body is something you need in order to stay
on this planet and you only get one.
And no matter which one you get, it will not
be satisfactory. It will not be beautiful
enough, it will not be fast enough, it will
not keep on for days at a time, but will
pull you down into a sleepy swamp and
demand apples and coffee and chocolate cake.
—Joyce Sutphen, "Living in the Body"

Iam always in a season of one kind or another.
Sometimes that season is time-related, physical and
clear—newborn or elderly or somewhere in between. Other
times I am less clear about my season. It is less physical
than emotional. I might be in my late forties, but there are
moments in which I feel far younger and moments in which I
feel far older. So I have these physical seasons that are strung
along like a timeline in the Farmer's Almanac, and then I
have seasonal moments that are hung like points on a chart,

dipping and reaching, high and low. There will be outlying points, of course, but for the most part, I live according to the season, and my body journeys with me along the way. It is as though each season offers a new version of that body—and they are all good. All bodies are good bodies, no matter the season.

In the life of the garden, I'm tempted to see one season as being better or worse than another. It feels impossible, sometimes, to simply live in that moment. It's a goal of mine to learn to embrace the garden in all of the seasons. I fail more often than not, but I want to be walking with some intention, looking for the beauty and the opportunity to give appropriate care for the garden for that moment. We don't sow spring seeds in the winter. The ground is too hard. We don't harvest before the bloom drops and the fruit ripens. Some days the care required is evident, but there are many times in which I may find I'm not sure what is needed. Identifying the season I'm in, physically, according to the timeline is not difficult. I look at a calendar for that. Those warm-weather moments within the winter or the cold snap in the spring, those are a bit trickier to navigate. I may be thrown off, or I may be delighted. It is the practice of being aware, being prayerful, being open, that helps me to walk through it no matter what may come.

If I can work toward seeing my season not as a limiting factor, but as a natural progression and process, I hope then

I will find the deeper gifts each season offers. If I can put aside the fraudulent messages I hear, or already hold onto, I hope I will find the gifts that emerge from the cold ground, all mystical and green, even in the winter of me. The beauty is astounding if I live according to the season, if I embrace the cycles of birth and death and rebirth: if I'm deep in the meaning and the wonder of the verdant spring, the sultry summer, the deep-hued autumn, and the holy winter.

 SPRING

The human body is God's wondrous creation, the most perfect creation in all nature.
—Fr. Alexander Men

IN THE SPRING everything is new, the ground is soft as the weather warms, and the rains come—unless you live in Chicago; then it's a gamble at best. The ground should be soft; the temperature should be warming. Sometimes it isn't. Sometimes it won't, at least at first. But it's the promise that keeps hope alive.

The house we owned in middle Tennessee had eighteen acres lined with dogwood trees. The first spring we lived there, we were blown away by the explosion of white dogwood flowers in early March. When we purchased the property, it was past the blooming season of the previous year. We had no idea the trees would flower. That first day of flowers was like magic, and I made the kids go outside with me to walk around exploring the newness of that place. We explored with wonder the soft, springy grass, the long limbs of the trees, the wet dirt and mud puddles.

For us city kids in the country, this was a new experience. I was not entirely sure how to guide the children. Do we venture into that rain-swollen stream? Do we swing from this long hanging branch? Is that wildlife safe? Exploration is the theme of childhood; parenting that band of explorers meant allowing for discovery. Spring is wonder, and spring is worry too.

The springtime body belongs to those early days of exploration and discovery. Newborn to infant, toddler to runner—each stage moves quickly, and yet there is a lengthening of days that mirrors that of the growing season. Each stage of development starts to stretch a bit longer as the awareness of our relationship to time grows. The springtime body undergoes more transformations than in any other time of our lives.

Imagine the look of the young, springtime garden, so full of possibility, so rich with hope for the future. The springtime version of us is that newly planted garden, delicate and yet gregarious. We hardly know what to do with the limbs one day, and then the next we are swinging from the low-hanging branches. Once we leave that springtime, it feels as though it was a million years from us. What happens in the transition between childhood and adolescence that creates that sense of disconnect?

"Her face is so changed," my friends say, when they see the pictures of my daughter between her first year and her third. Her legs are longer, her arms are stronger, her teeth are filling in the gaps, and she talks all the time. She talks in a constant chatter—noticing and commenting and taking it in. From three to five years old, her arms and legs stretch further, her head is filled with learning new things, new words, new actions. She runs, she jumps, she climbs trees. She reaches toward nine and then ten, her movements are more deliberate but still a kind of wilderness. She is the epitome of the springtime. She is at the start of the blooming season. She is wild but controlled, still very much in the growing season. I can still see the soil between her toes.

The springtime body is new. I see it modeled on this beautiful new person in my house. From where I sit, far from my own springtime body, knowing the seasons ahead, I delight in these springtime moments. I breathe them deep, like the sweet, clean air I had almost forgotten. Breathing that air brings me right back to that season, to that forgotten spring.

Each shift from one season to another brings a kind of forgetting. Breathing the moments when I recognize them, appreciate them, welcome them is remembering. It is most evident in the move from the springtime to adolescence because the changes are so very physical, and they so often come with emotional swings. Growth spurts at the spring-time stage are focused on foundational things—learning to walk, talk, run, and sing, moving toward the bloom of the summertime body. This is simply the natural progression of things. I forgot my springtime body because it was so much about function, caught in the constant theme of change. I leave behind a version of that springtime body, it seems, every few months, or at least every year—but I want to remember it. I want to hold it close, to thank it for the hard work of growing and changing and learning new things, new words, new actions.

 SUMMER

In summer, the song sings itself.
—William Carlos Williams

THE LOOK OF THE WELL-NURTURED summer garden can be stunning. The colors are vibrant; the aroma of the flowers is enchanting. As with every season, every cycle of life, there are transitions here too. The changes are rapid, and yet at the same time, it's a natural impulse to feel as though we are pulled in two directions, reaching back into childhood and the familiar, and then reaching forward into adulthood and the unknown.

Adolescence is terrifying. We are bursting forth—body and mind. We shoot up like young bamboo, overnight. We blossom and break out and feel as though at any moment a new world might explode from out of our ribcage. In the summer cycle of the body, we are vulnerable even in our blooming. I can see it now, from the safety of my current season. I can see the vulnerability, though I tried hard to hide it under bulky sweaters and jeans cut off at the knees.

It is amazing to me how I still cling to the image of the body I had in this time of my life. I look at photos of the summertime self and wonder how I squandered that. I wonder how I can possibly return to it. I admit that I kept my summertime body weight the same on my driver's license long after the summertime faded into the autumn. It was a strange day, almost empowering, to have to say, when asked whether anything had changed, that yes, I was now a new arbitrary number for that piece of plastic. The empowerment was an admission that I was in a new season. The admission was a relief. I was setting aside the old notion of who I thought I was supposed to be and moving into the new version I carried, and it was good—or at least it was all right.

But I still look at those summertime pictures. I see that young woman on the verge of some new and exciting life. When we are in the springtime, we encounter our bodies as an integrated whole, bumbling around the world. It is us, together, and then everything outside of us. We do not think to see the body as separate at that time in our lives.

It is here, in the summertime, when the emotions run high, the body shifts into new horizons, and our social lives and school lives and home lives start to feel overwhelming that we tend to stand apart from everything else. We start to compare what we see in the media, at school, at work, in our friends and even our family with the body we see in the mirror. Studies report that in this season of life, both boys and girls begin to give in to the messages that surround them about how they "ought" to look physically, and I believe it. I remember that. We step into that new phase of life, with heightened emotions, added responsibilities, bombarded by images and admonishments in a season that really ought to be about admiring the beauty of the garden, the flowers in bloom, the tree branches reaching up with their wild green boughs. Instead, we get bogged down, ready to pull out the plants from their roots without even knowing why.

It is here, in the summertime season of the garden, that I formed bad behaviors and attitudes toward my body. I integrated these images and messages, and I carried them around with me into adulthood. Sometimes those behaviors and attitudes were confronted later; sometimes they were not. I let them live there in my pockets until they soaked into my skin and bled into my bloodstream. The irony that I would look back on that summertime season, wistful and wishing, is clear. I am filled with "if only." If only I had known what I know now. If only I had appreciated that body. If only I had thought to pay better attention.

I want to wrap that summertime girl in my arms now and tell her it's all going to be okay. I want to hold her, though she will squirm at the holding. I won't be able to convince her, though. I know it. Summertime is about blooming, bright and brilliant. I cannot keep that summertime girl protected. I cannot go back and do it better. I cannot go back to the summertime body. But I can look at those days and unpack the messages I picked up. I can pull the weeds that grow and choke the good messages, the ones that come from the One who made me, the One who sees how lovely that garden is and has always been.

> For You formed my inward parts;
> You covered me in my mother's womb.
> I will praise You, for I am fearfully and wonderfully made;
> Marvelous are Your works,
> And that my soul knows very well.
> (Psalm 139:13–14)

His works are wonderful, and I am a work of His making. I wish it were a simple action, a simple shift back to being content in the current season. In the summertime cycle of the body, I might not have gotten that reminder as often as I needed. It's not too late to hear that reminder now, every day, to soften the hard thatched places, the wild grown-over places, the dormant and waiting places in that garden.

In the summertime of the body, I am living in the tension of the loss of the springtime and the promise of the autumn, living in the bloom of the garden and yet always reminded that the autumn is coming. If we are fortunate, we have moments in this summertime in which we can just rest in the beauty of this garden. This is the gift of the summertime body, and it is the memory of this that comes back to comfort me—and maybe to challenge, too, in the autumn and in the winter.

But there is something else. There is an urgency as well for those of us who are already living in the autumn body or the winter body. We have a responsibility here to the next generation of women and men coming through their summertime. This means that we become aware of our own season, for our own good, but also for the good of the summertime people who surround us. I consider here the words of encouragement and care that were or would have been foundational to me in my summertime. I can still see the summertime around me, no matter which season I live in now. Rather than looking back at my own spring and summer and lamenting the transition, maybe it's more my task to embrace the gifts of those seasons and offer cultivation to the people around me who might not be inclined to see, as clearly or easily, the vibrancy and beauty.

AUTUMN

No spring nor summer's beauty hath such grace
As I have seen in one Autumnal face.

—John Donne, "Elegy IX: The Autumnal"

FORTY IS THE NEW THIRTY and thirty is the new black. They say it looks good on everyone. It's slimming and never goes out of style. I got pregnant for the first time when I was thirty. There was no slimming happening there. I gained fifty-two pounds without even batting an eye. It was the first time I didn't think about the food I ate or how much I moved. I loved my growing belly, my shifting hips, my lumbering along that third trimester. My doctor was "crunchy"; he thought women should pay less attention to their weight while pregnant and focus on growing a healthy baby, so I took him at his word and delighted in being pregnant. It might have been the first time in my life I didn't worry about gaining weight. Though I had a slim build in my summertime body, I still carried around the fear that I ought to be concerned about "getting fat."

These messages surround me; they press in when I least expect it. Some messages come from friends or family members. Some come from advertising and television shows I watch. It's impossible to escape the onslaught. Still, there was a freedom in that season of the body, the one that housed four children over the course of my thirties.

At this writing, I am heavier than I have ever been, apart from those times when I was pregnant or thereabouts. I won't lie. I miss my springtime and summertime body—the version of this body I had when I was younger. I still remember well the long, smooth limbs of myself as a sapling. I wonder how on earth I ever found complaint about that body. It was strong and steady, lithe and ready to move. I moved without pain then. Now, every new pain is a reminder that this is not my spring body. This is my autumn body, transitional and changing again all the time.

The challenge of the autumn season depends on the planting of the spring and the summer. The chorus of "if only I had known" starts as a whisper here. In the autumn I start to see the effects of gravity and time. I may still think, in moments, that I'm in the summertime body. Perhaps, given good genes and planning, some are still there, but for me, this is the season in which I settle into an uneasy partnership with my body.

This is the season of sliding into winter without really thinking about it. This is the season in which I want to slow down the process, perhaps for the first time. The springtime and the summer of us want to constantly be on the move, want to reach forward like creeping myrtle covering the bare open areas. There is much to explore, much to become, much to bloom. But in the autumn, we're digging roots deeper, preparing for the winter but not stationary—not yet.

Though the autumn body can feel as transitional as the spring or the summer, I am also reaching back, trying to turn back the clock, trying to keep that long slide into winter at bay for as long as possible. And yet, it is beautiful here, too. In some places the season shift at autumn is incredible, reds and golds taking the place of the green of spring and summer. I can see that I am colorful at this stage, not from the blooming of the flowers and fruits, but from the actual clothing of this tree. What a tremendous thing to know that possibility, that color I hold. And then the tree starts to shed that brilliant cloth, dropping its leafy robe to the ground, covering the soil below softly, and the wind blows and carries it through the yards and the streets. It is as though the world has been enveloped with the gift of those leaves.

What then does this say of us, in our autumn shift? We are no longer in the springtime, focused on the growing and development of the body. We are no longer in the summer, focused on the blooming of our selves. No, here we are in the harvest—child-bearing, career-building, child-rearing, neighboring, care-taking, leaf-scattering. Here, in the autumn, we reach with all our leaf-baring branches into the world around us. This body, this autumn body, is full and giving. It is tragic when we overlook that truth for the vapid lie we hear, that we "ought" to be thinner or richer or have poutier lips. If we're willing in this autumn body to see, instead, the reds and the golds that we're sending into the streets, the yards, the oceans, the mountainside—can you imagine the possibilities of that? What far-reaching place will you go with the gifts of this season?

I cannot say enough about the beauty of the autumn, mine and yours and all of ours. As with all seasons, it is in motion. As with all seasons, it is a gift. If this is where you are at this moment, take it in. Admire the beauty of this season. Admire the strength of this body, the persistence, the wholeness, the balance of the Spirit of God that informs it and the treasure that you bring to the people around you. Those leaves will scatter, cushioning the earth for warmth in winter.

 WINTER

You have set all the borders of the earth;
You have made summer and winter.

(Psalm 74:17)

WHEN IT IS WINTER, I'm not thinking about the garden. In some ways, I am already relieved for the autumn to be over. I am sitting and watching the snow fall, the flakes piling up on the covered deck furniture, the leaves I neglected to rake given a blanket until the snow melts. I am not thinking about what I ought to do to prepare for the spring. More likely, I am fixated on what I neglected to do before that snow fell. It is the falling of that snow that reminds me of all the things left undone, because I know at that moment how much harder it will be when the spring comes.

My gardener friend, Mary, told me years ago that she planted garlic every fall. She'd plant a variety of garlic bulbs at the end of one growing season in preparation for another that was still far away. I admire that forethought. I find I am always playing catch-up. To plan ahead like that seems unlikely, but each year when September rolls around, I resurrect this idea about growing garlic that has been long buried throughout the spring growing season. It has been long buried through the summer while I fight the heat and the insects. It has been long buried when I stand in the produce aisle and stare at the one type of fresh garlic bulbs I am offered. *I can grow this,* I think to myself, *if I plan ahead.*

But I don't plan ahead, and then in September I am scrambling to complete the basic tasks necessary to close out the dying window boxes. I am pulling weeds that got by me all summer. I am buying school supplies for children returning to school. I am planning meals that adapt to new schedules and sports-related extracurriculars. I have no time to devote to the spring. I can only think of now.

It might be a phase. I tell myself this as I am staring at the falling snow and remembering that this was the year I intended to have the gutters cleaned out before the winter came. I tell myself this as I'm remembering that I intended to plant garlic this year, finally. I wanted to be able to see something green sprout up in my raised bed on the patio and pat myself on the back for that small victory.

It's not so terrible to recognize one's limitations in life circumstances. We're all in a season of one sort or another. It's not the recognition of the seasons that bothers me but the shame I impose on myself when I catch a glimpse in the mirror and see how the season is taking shape on my neck or my thighs or my belly. I try to remember that this aging process is natural. I want to embrace that process. I want to love the body I've been given care of without judgment in those moments when I remember that I had intended to walk more while it was warm, to eat local and fresh in the dewy springtime, to breathe the air of a countryside once in a while, and take advantage of the new bike trail the city opened this past summer.

I am conflicted then. I want to have walked into this new season prepared and ready for whatever comes next, and yet now as I watch the snow fall I can only see the leaves I did not rake, the bulbs I did not plant. I feel I am lacking. I feel I am failing. It's a terrible way to start a season.

I'm not here yet, in the winter. I'm still wading deep in the autumn leaves scattered at my feet. Even so, I am thinking about how to wrap those leaves around my trunk and roots to keep me warm when things turn colder. As with all seasons, I cannot know what the winter will hold for me. So much seems as though it depends on the now—drink more water, take the stairs, eat more kale. And so much seems to depend on genetics and heredity and things I have little to no control over anymore. What will the winter look like when it greets me? How can I imagine it? Should I imagine it?

It is here that I rely, once again, on the words of the saints, both living and long gone. I look in particular to the saints who dwell close to my heart—St. Isaac, St. Ephrem, St. Tikhon:

> We see the water of a river flowing uninterruptedly and passing away, and all that floats on its surface, rubbish or beams of trees, all pass by. Christian! So does our life. . . . I was an infant, and that time has gone. I was an adolescent, and that too has passed. I was a young man, and that too is far behind me. The strong and mature man that I was is no more. My hair turns white, I succumb to age, but that too passes; I approach the end and will go the way of all flesh. I was born to die. I die that I may live. Remember me, O Lord, in Thy Kingdom!
>
> —St. Tikhon of Voronezh

And I look, too, to living saints, people who walk alongside and have seen the road ahead, whether I relate to them in person over coffee or through their written works. I am most drawn to the work of poets. There is a gift in poetry that I cannot explain with any real adequacy. Poetry winds its way into my soul. It says volumes in only the briefest of language. The words my favorite poets put on paper are like super-powerful multivitamins for the human condition.

In her book *The Adventure of Ascent,* poet Luci Shaw describes, almost as in a journal, her experience with this winter season. She draws imagery from nature, from the body, from her long life lived through the lens of poetry and a love of language.

> *A winter garden is a pretty sad place, drab and brown with rotting leaves and twigs, destitute of green and growth but for the moss that somehow thrives even after being frozen. It velvets over the harshness of the granite boulders around which our native plants are artfully arranged.*
>
> *Today, Liz, our "gardening angel" who has been overseeing the garden's health and welfare for several months, came to groom and trim. The sun actually shone at a low angle, and the sky brightened after the days of heavy rain that had turned our creek into a wild, foaming cascade below the garden. Liz cut back the dark, dead upright stems of the ornamental grasses, the crocosmia, astrancia and peonies, and pruned the potentilla.*
>
> *At this time of year it's sometimes possible to see tiny green buds on certain bushes. It's the increased light that prompts the green to grow. Light equals life.*

When Luci Shaw speaks of this wintertime garden, she does not pull punches with her assessment of it. She does not gloss over the realities of aging here. She does not advocate for avoiding or tossing away the wintertime garden, but rather instructs us to pay attention. This is the particular gift of poets, this paying attention.

In the winter of ourselves, we have gathered the benefit of our years. We are a collection of stories and seeds. It is a goal of mine to be more like Luci Shaw as I enter into the wintertime, seeing all that is there to be seen, telling the stories I have stored so carefully over the course of this fragile lifetime. I am paying attention and noticing things as small and seemingly insignificant as the green of the moss in the midst of winter. It's all about seeing the light. As Luci tells us, "Light equals life."

We reach these seasons whether we do what we intended to do or not. Time moves apart from us. It has no care of us. The winter comes on a calendar, and of course it will catch us unprepared. I often feel as though I had no control over how or what I chose in the lead-up to the snowfall, but then I take it apart a little and remember how that past season truly did unfold—I did not plant those garlic bulbs because I was busy doing something else. I did not go for walks because my husband was ill. I did not pay attention to the changing of the seasons because the weather was odd, or the dust was too thick on the bookshelf one day, and it distracted me until I remedied it.

I will be busy doing other things. I will get lost in the dailyness of my human life. I will ignore the needs or goals of my physical body. Sometimes I am disconnected from myself. The winter comes, and regret takes up the space that was meant for rest or peace. I know that regret has its

84

place. I regret the not planning ahead and the lack of care I give myself. It's important for me to remember, though, that regret is not a stopping point but a beginning. It is an opportunity to turn again toward the goal. Just because I missed the chance to plant the bulbs or take the walks does not negate the goal. It does not cancel out my chance to become healthy and whole. There is still time. There is still garlic. There is still light sneaking into the garden. How do I remember to look there for it? How to I recognize that light and follow it to the small patch of green moss that reminds me that life is still working here?

The regret is most pressing to me after I catch that look in the mirror that reminds me that I've forgotten myself. I try to make a new choice out of that immediate regret. I have to force myself to stop the flow of criticism I want to offer. I talk out loud to myself in the mirror, like a teacher giving instruction to a student: "No, not like that," I say, "be gentle with yourself. Remember the season."

I want to remember, especially in the winter, the cycles of these things. It is not always this cold; the trees are not stuck forever with bare limbs. Spring will come, and things will bloom again. I cannot plant myself in the regret based on the incomplete picture the mirror offers. I am more than that picture. I am more than the thighs that gain and lose muscle and fat. I am more than the skin dotted with blemishes. I am more than the soil waiting for the seeds to be planted.

In that small space of time after catching the glimpse of the body in the mirror, or in watching the snow fall on gutters piled with leaves, or in raised beds that missed the chance for planted bulbs, we are offered the chance to receive and then offer a new perspective—no matter the season or condition, we are created good, *Imago Dei,* icons of Christ. There is still light here. This is foundational, unchanging, and true. So we have the chance in this moment to be gentle with ourselves, to give praise to God for this remarkable gift of life, whether or not we took the walks we hoped to take or planted the bulbs we hoped to plant—and that's important.

Here, take a breath, give thanks, it's good, we're good. I give thanks because I find that gratitude cures a great many ills. When, in response to regret, I move away from shame and toward gratitude, I am building the foundation for whatever I encounter next. That is the miracle of this moment. That is the reaching toward God that will help to guide me through, no matter how often I feel unprepared for the changes that come in this over-wintering, which is always. Rather than dwell in thinking I "should have" eaten better or exercised more, it's important to take a moment, to take stock, to remind myself once again that I am more than the sum of my body parts. Though our body may have entered into the winter of our years physically, on an emotional and spiritual level we are still engaging in the seasons. In this sense, there will be another spring, another summer, another autumn, another winter. There is time to attend to each of the needs of this garden in each season. The winter isn't the end of us.

If each physical and spiritual season brings with it a new set of challenges, a new list of things to do as well as ways to be, then within each cycle we are inclined to revisit the insecurities of that season. But let's consider that each season of the body offers us a "new" version of the garden. Can we recall the beauty inherent in this version? The garden is just as colorful in the reds and golds of autumn as in the violets and greens of spring, just as rich while dressed in the muted hues of winter as in the warm palette of summer. No matter what our season of life, no matter what our condition, or our transitions or blossoming—this is our garden, and it is beautiful, in every season.

CHAPTER SIX

PLANTINGS

On Testimonials

Just as painters in working from models constantly gaze at their exemplar and thus strive to transfer the expression of the original to their own artistry, so too he who is anxious to make himself perfect in all kinds of virtue must gaze upon the lives of the saints . . . and must make their excellence his own by imitation.

— St. Basil the Great

The large back deck of the loft we rented in Chicago for a year or so offered a beautiful view of the majestic skyline in the distance. In the near view, however, it hung over the alley behind the building, and across the alley was a line of pallet yards. All day long, trucks would come down that alley and idle there. Sounds of the workers filled the air, along with the exhaust that poured from the tailpipes of those trucks. But at night, when the pallet yards were closed and the trucks were gone, the air felt clean at last, the lights of the city were inviting. In order to make that space feel somewhat hospitable despite the daytime near view, we bought a nice set of outdoor furniture and some decent lighting, and I tried to fill the space with plants. I decided I'd also try my hand at growing an herb garden outside from seed.

It had been a couple of weeks since the seeds went into the soil, and I was waiting. I thought I'd gotten the timing right, consulted a garden fanatic friend, the almanac, the Internet, the back of the seed pack I bought at the grocery store. When I told my garden fanatic friend I had purchased seeds at the grocery store, she developed a sort of nervous facial tic, but knowing me as she does, she chose not to lecture on the particulars. She understood that for me, just attempting to grow anything at all is a challenge. I think she let it go in an effort to keep me moving forward in spite of my mediocre seed choice. I value that grace. In moments like that, and friendships like ours, I recognize the gift in a push toward progress rather than perfection.

I watched that patch of soil every day, checking it as I left the house in the morning to take the kids to school. Checking it as I came back into the house. Checking it in the afternoon when the sun was at its height, when the dew was finally dry, when the neighbors or the pallet-yard workers weren't around to catch me talking to the yet unhatched seeds sitting there dormant just a quarter of an inch under the surface of the planter. "Come on along, fellas," I'd say, "come on along." But there was nothing to show for it. All that prep and timing and patience—and thus far, I could spy nothing.

It might have been the squirrels digging in that box just a few hours after my planting. I had repaired the damage as much as I was able. More likely it was the sudden and unexpected dip in temperatures that one night after I planted those tiny seeds just below the surface of the soil. I tried to picture them there under the blanket of dirt, warm and content, just biding their time. Seeds have an inner knowledge of time and temperature. They store an ancient memory inside. They contain all the elements necessary to grow into herbs and flowering plants, bushes and trees. Seeds are remarkable and miraculous. Given the proper environment, nurturing, and guidance, they produce new life.

We have this inner planting happening, this ancient memory inside, waiting for the right moment, waiting for the time and the temperature to trigger us. We plant this garden often without thinking, without planning. But seeds are delicate, too, deserving of attention and care. If we think of ourselves as the garden, then we have to think also about the soil and about the seeds and about the nurturing and the guidance. And we have to be patient.

The first tender shoots that finally came up that spring were glorious to behold. They seemed to defy the environment they were entering, and that was hopeful. It is hard to imagine that something so small can burst forth new life out of the soil even with my lacking gardener's skills. The inner workings of it are wondrous, and yet they are still, on some level, mechanical too.

There are scores of books about the biology of how a seed becomes a plant, how a sapling grows into a tree. It's a network of events, a symphony we do not see conducted. There are actions we put into motion the moment we decide to put that seed into the ground. We have to be willing to learn, willing to prepare, and then willing to wait. One does not have to be a master gardener to start a new planting, but it helps to know the basics, and it helps to have some guidance. The more we know about the function of the plants, the better we can care for the tender shoots when they appear.

The same is true of the body. Knowing the way the body functions leads us into a deeper appreciation of the miracle of this garden, the wonder of its workings; but having some example helps too. Seeing the gardens of neighbors and friends, wandering the Botanic Garden in Chicago, seeing pictures in the catalogues. This helps bridge the gap between the now and the not yet. It's encouraging and it's inspiring. I need this.

You must allow yourself to approach silently nearer and nearer to yourself: the past, the present and the future in this moment of silence . . . all the waters of your life which

*flow away and run out and which are collected in the one
basin of a heart aware of itself.*

—Fr. Karl Rahner

AT FIRST GLANCE, the rules of doctrine and practice for the
Orthodox Faith can seem intense. There are shelves, perhaps entire libraries, dedicated to the rule of the Church—
how to pray, how to fast, how to be attentive, how to read
the calendar and adhere to the fast and feast days. If I'm not
careful, I can spend too much time focused on the rule—the
more cerebral parts of this religious practice. I can miss the
forest through the trees.

The first thing I learned as a catechumen, in that time
of learning about the Orthodox Faith, was that I could not
understand Orthodoxy by simply reading about it. I had to
attend, I had to enter in, and that was overwhelming. It's
one thing to learn about the practices of a tradition from
the safety of my armchair; it's another to do it in front of a
group of new people gathered together for that purpose.

There was an element of belonging that I was seeking
when I became Orthodox. Walking into Liturgy for the first
time, alone and unsure of what to do next, feels an awful lot
like walking into a new gym or an exercise class for the first
time, or the second, or even the third and beyond. It can
be intimidating. How do I know if I'm doing it right? Will
I be judged harshly if I'm doing it wrong? Will I be injured
in the process? The second-guessing and the intimidation

can be enough to keep me out of the Liturgy and out of the gym or the exercise class. It is in confronting those fears that I find the benefit of the practice. It is uncomfortable. So while the rules and guidelines of the Church are invaluable to me in theory, it is in the living out of those rules that I truly see change happen. I push through it—I have to—but I'm not always happy to do it.

I often complain that I wish the fictional "think method" Professor Henry Hill used in *The Music Man* would actually work in real life, especially in the area of exercise and eating. I would think about doing a workout and eating well all day long, and wake up to find the benefits of that method in the morning. Of course, I know in reality that it is the doing of those things that will take me further, but it's hard to wait. It's hard to trust that the end result will meet the goals I set. It's hard to hope that what I aim for, the picture on the front of the seed pack, will come to pass eventually.

This is why before-and-after photos are so convincing to those of us who want to look to pills or methods for toning up or spot-reducing or clearing up our adult acne. I like to see that someone else has done it first and that it works. I'll take the testimonials of people who have gone before. I look to them as a sort of authority when I don't know whether I ought to buy what the company is selling. Many of us fall into that trap because we have good intentions, we have high hopes, but we're not entirely sure how to get to where we want to be.

So my issue with the testimonials is this: I want good results, but I'm looking at the wrong set of standards from the start—the unattainable "after" picture. If I set up the goal based upon the before-and-after pictures I see around me, it can feel as though I'm failing already. Before-and-after photos do not tell us the whole story of a person's journey. In some cases, the testimonials are true and the teller is trustworthy. In some cases, they are not—lighting, posture, body position, even the difference between a smile on one's face in the "after" and a scowl in the "before" will give the impression of progress. Everyone has a story: a tale about the diet that worked wonders, the herb that cured that round of gout, the neighbor who swears by the supplements she got online; but the goal is the thing. Goals based on the pallet yard at night, when all is quiet and calm, the lights of the city in the distance, give me an incomplete picture. Things are not always what they seem. Shortsighted goals will bring short-lived results.

But what endures? What will pass the test of time? Whose story can I trust? Going it alone or employing the "think method" won't get me far on the road. Comparing myself to the marketing materials around me only plants seeds of discouragement and envy that will choke the progress of this garden.

Abba Poemen said that Abba John said that the saints are like a group of trees, each bearing different fruit, but watered from the same source. The practices of one saint differ from those of another, but it is the same Spirit that works in all of them.

—Benedicta Ward, *The Sayings of the Desert Fathers*

I CANNOT KNOW ABOUT THE CHURCH until I enter in. When I am afraid to enter in, I look to the lives of the saints for some motivation. The lives of the saints, whether living or long gone—they are the guides. If the Church provides the doctrinal guidelines for our spiritual lives—the "rule," as it were—the lives of the saints provide the testimonials to their efficacy. In the lives of the saints, we see their struggles and their hardships—which feel something like a version of our struggles and our hardships—and the evidence of the rule they chose to put into action. There is some comfort in knowing that those who have gone ahead of us have been challenged and come out of it with some greater understanding about the nature of God and man in communion.

In a way, the icons I see on the walls of my Orthodox church become a kind of "after" picture to the stories of each saint. We are, after all, living icons of Christ—all of us. The word *icon* comes from the Greek word *eikona*, meaning "image" or "likeness." We are the image and likeness of the One who has made us.

On a spiritual level, I look to the lives of the saints not

to shame me into attending Liturgy or living a better life, but to remember that I have a connection to those who have gone before. I don't have to live in a hermitage engaged in the strict ascetic life of the Desert Fathers. They've done that work. I have their stories to show what endures despite the noisy, pollution-filled near view of the alley below. The saints have laid groundwork, given words of wisdom and inspiration. The story they leave behind is meant to show that we are family, that we are not alone. They show that we can find the joy that comes with struggle, in spite of the circumstances. The seeds will break the surface of the soil with time and care—not a quick fix, not a thirty-day cleanse, but attention and consistency.

When my daughter was very young, she had bad dreams. She would crawl into my bed looking for comfort. She would lie awake, even then, and worry about the dream. My groggy responses were of some consolation, I suppose, as she kept waking me up if I fell asleep before she finally nodded off. After a few nights of sleep deprivation, I counseled her to pray in the middle of the night when she felt afraid. Despite my best efforts, she would still crawl into my bed, or, if I took her back to her room, she'd call from her bed night after night until I'd go in to comfort her. When I asked if she prayed first, she said, "Yes, but I want real arms to hug me!" and I get that. I understand that need for real arms to hold me, that strong sense of belonging to a place and a people. In our physical lives, community is meant to help us along the way.

Fellow travelers are those real arms to hug us and encourage us. The lives of the saints—both the historical saints and the everyday saints, the ones who walk through the doorway of the church, or the gym, the grocery store, even our homes—can be my best source of support. They are the people who will look at the garden in the dead of winter or the massive rain and flood and see the small herb shoots that spring up in opposition to the noisy, exhaust-filled alley. They are the ones we can turn to when we're most afraid. They will remind us in whispers and calm confidence of the beauty we hold—*Just wait. Be patient. Don't give up. You're doing it right. You're worthy and loved.*

The words of the ones who have gone before us show the path forward. They offer the almanac of care for the garden—things that do not change with time or cultural trends and "breakthrough" diet plans. The everyday saints, the people who walk alongside, offer the real arms and the soft voices that bolster us toward the long-term changes we hope to see. This is the real "before and after" we yearn to see.

So the lives of the saints who are long gone make a historical foundation. They show it *can* be done, despite the odds. And the lives of the living saints who stand next to me in the pew, the grocery store, the living room, or the gym are the functional working out of that foundation. We can trust these testimonials, because they're borne out over time in the stories of those who have come before us, and in real life as well—in the relationships with living saints we choose for our daily lives. It is the connection to those who have gone before and the connection to those who surround us now—those real arms to wrap around us—that moves us forward in our progress—physical, emotional, or spiritual. We need *this* sort of testimonial to keep the garden healthy in growing seasons, in fallow seasons, in drought, in flood, in harvest.

CHAPTER SEVEN

WATERING

On Connection and Comparison

The LORD WILL GUIDE YOU CONTINUALLY,
And satisfy your soul in drought,
And strengthen your bones;
You shall be like a watered garden,
And like a spring of water, whose waters do not fail.
(Isaiah 58:11)

In late 2000, we moved from a house with a small city-sized yard in Chicago to a spread of eighteen acres in the middle of rural Tennessee. The children were still small. Their ages—one, three, five, and eight—made the transition simple in some ways. They were happy for the change to fresh air and room to run. I was happy for a little breathing room as well.

We had plans for the acreage. We hoped to build a garden there, sprawling and wild but fruitful and beautiful too. In the midst of this transition, we brought in a professional landscaper to give her impressions of the area, and to draw up some plans for the garden and the overall feel of the outdoor area near the house.

While surrounded by trees on all sides as far as the eye could see, the house itself was in a clearing, set apart, as though in the middle of a pasture. It stood alone there, hemmed in by nature on all sides. We could not see a neighbor's house when the leaves were on the trees. Only in winter, when the trees were bare, did we spy a light in the distance, or maybe smoke from a bonfire or chimney. We were alone, and when the children were asleep, it was quiet. I loved the quiet, and the slow pace, and the isolation—for a while.

Once the designs were drawn up, the cost of bringing them to fruition came in, and we began to see the cracks in the plan. Water was one problem that cropped up. We were on a well out there, and a large garden meant a need for a good irrigation system. We didn't have the resources we needed to make it work. The reality of the cost, plus the time it would take to get the construction done, get the garden planted and flourishing, not to mention the time to tend the garden and tend the children while my husband traveled for work, was overwhelming. It undid the quiet of the country. It pressed in on us so much that we halted the plan, waiting for a better time to start.

For five years we considered the garden, we went back to the plans again and again, but the time never seemed right. The longer we spent in the middle of nowhere, far from our Chicago community, far from neighbors and schools and grocery stores, the more the isolation weighed on our family. I was alone too much, with only pint-sized companions and a complement of my anxious thoughts to keep me company. The isolation was crippling. It crept in quietly on spring days and summer evenings, it floated in on rustling autumn leaves, it watched from the bare arms of the winter trees. The isolation, being alone and afraid, was painful—but not a sharp knife-like pain. It was a dull ache in the pit of the stomach. Loneliness is like that. It shuts us down. It dries us out.

To finally surrender ourselves to healing, we have to have three spaces opened up within us—and all at the same time: our opinionated head, our closed-down heart, and our defensive and defended body. That is the summary work of spirituality—and it is indeed work.
—Richard Rohr

THERE ARE A NUMBER OF REASONS I do not care for hospitals. The fact that I spent a length of time in one when I was very young figures in on a deep level. I do not remember that hospital stay because I was only eighteen months old, but I think my body remembers it. I think my psyche remembers it. Sometimes I try to imagine what that small girl felt, lying in the bed at night with the lights blinking, strange smells, machines beeping, and people walking in muffled shoe sounds while I tried to sleep. My mother told me I would cry when she left, so she devised a system of carrying two purses when she'd come. One was a decoy purse. She would leave that one in my sight so I would know she was coming back, even if it meant she was coming back after a night of beeping machines and blinking lights without her.

Even now, the nighttime is a strange and silent time. I have trouble dropping off to sleep in my own bed. I have trouble shutting off my brain and just letting the day go, finally. It is as though I need the daytime to leave its purse on a table nearby so I know it is returning. Comfort comes in connection, knowing we are not alone.

After I fell on the ski slope and tore the ligament in my knee, I visited an orthopedic surgeon to get his take on the issue. He suggested I have it repaired. He suggested that as I aged it would be better to have strong knees. And he said that my joints were, as he put it, "loosey goosey," which is inner-circle medical jargon, obviously. He said repairing the ligament would be a benefit to me in the long run, and so I swallowed my apprehension and had the work done. It was supposed to be outpatient surgery, but I had trouble with the IV, and so they used a general anesthesia. I had trouble coming out of the sedation. After the surgery, I lay in the recovery room trying to shake off the sedation, feeling increasingly groggy, nauseated, and headachy. I watched as other patients were wheeled in for recovery and then released. I waited and watched, feeling the conflicting emotions of wanting to leave and yet wanting to sleep.

The doctor decided to keep me overnight just to be sure I was all right. They moved me to another room, and though I was hopped up on pain pills, I could not sleep that night. I was cold, lonely, sick, and in pain. I was a mess. By the time my husband came to get me the next morning, I was torn apart by the pain meds and anesthesia hangover. I wanted to go home, and I did not want to move. Despite the strong desire to be warm at home in my own bed, I did not want to deal with the transition of going home. I just wanted to be there already.

I think the worst part about being in the hospital overnight, freezing and in pain, was that I was alone in unfamiliar territory. Apart from the night nurse, who'd scuttle in from time to time while I pretended to sleep, I was missing connection and comfort, and that made everything worse. When the surgeon came in to give me the release to go home, he asked a series of questions about how I felt, whether there was pain, where I felt the pain, how bad it hurt, and the like. It was hard to answer. As I consider it now, I realize how detached I felt from my body and from that whole surgical experience. I was stuck in the discomfort of that moment and desperate to be somewhere else, somewhere better, physically and emotionally. When the doctor asked about the pain, I could not quite identify it because I was shut down. I was already yearning for the next, more comfortable moment.

Comparison is the thief of joy.

—Eleanor Roosevelt

THE GARDEN GIVES SIGNALS when it is in need. When a garden needs water, the leaves will wilt, and the blooms will grow dull or look washed out. The body gives signals too—feelings of hunger, pain, and perhaps loneliness certainly make us aware that we are in need. I miss the signals sometimes. I'm not always paying attention. But when the leaves begin to drop, I want to gather myself in, I want to develop this body and soul awareness.

When I ask myself, "How do I know if I am okay?" I'm apt to look externally at how everyone else is doing, how everyone else is moving and recovering. I think to myself, *I should be better. I should be further along the road*. I know that in those moments, what I want is connection and comfort. What I resort to is comparison and then discontent. I'm inclined to look at the other gardens around me to gauge my progress or my worth, and this can be dangerous.

When I look outward, to others' successes and failures, I get out my emotional measuring tape to see how I stack up against them. It's exhausting to measure myself against the people who walk alongside, not to mention the people I see in magazines and on television, have never met or hope to meet. Comparison tries to convince me that it is there for my own good. *Here is the mark; aim here,* it says. But that mark is off center, or too high, or perhaps too low, or in another country altogether. It makes no sense to compare apples to street lamps, but I do it anyway. Force of habit.

I want to know that I'm doing what I am supposed to do to reach the goals I set. When I don't see the number on the scale move or the symptoms decrease, when I don't see my thighs shape up or skin clear according to the schedule other people hit, I wonder what I'm doing wrong. I wonder about these things because I'm comparing my results to the ones I see in the magazine article or to the neighbor who made an incredible transformation. I compare my progress to the story I heard once about the guy who cured his asthma by eating only bee pollen for three weeks or the claims made by people around me about the miracles and wonders of this fad or that trend.

Comparison is the thief of joy, ultimately, because comparisons work against our good design. This kind of comparison works against the love and compassion required for me to live well in communion with my bodily self, my spiritual life, and my community. Comparison sneaks in and tells me terrible lies about the state of my affairs—that I am falling short, or perhaps that I am rising high above the rooftops. Whether it is saying I am better than or less than, comparison sets up a false standard, a destructive phantom competition. When I don't win that competition, I feel envious. I want to tear down the other or tear down myself. Comparison paves the road for envy, and envy drives down that road to injury. So I cannot live alone, isolated and fading away, and I cannot live a life of comparison. Where does that leave me?

※※※※※※※

In the beginning, envy is revealed through inappropriate zeal and rivalry, and later by fervor with spite and the blaming of the one who is envied.
—St. Ambrose of Optina

IF I TAKE A MOMENT HERE, I can consider the many varied body types, styles, colors, and shapes of the human form. What a remarkable product line we have here in humanity, allowing for a wide range of diversity. The garden of humanity is full and vibrant—brilliant trees, flowers, vines, and ground cover. I remind myself there is no one perfect physical standard, and to think otherwise is to fall into thinking everyone else is inherently flawed.

If I can begin to truly see the people around me as icons of the One who made us, reflections of the Creator, it might short-circuit this unhealthy habit of comparison. It might transform the envy to wonder, awe, appreciation. Instead of wandering the gardens around me and moving to tear them down or tear myself down because of the differences, perhaps compassion will grow. Compassion, from the Latin, meaning "to suffer with." We *suffer with* one another, knowing that we are not alone in our pain, our sadness, our wishing for being more or better. It may be in this knowing, this connection that we finally see the beauty in the gardens that surround us. We ought to drink that in, build that up, and store it away for the times when we are alone and wondering if we're okay. Perhaps compassion is a kind of cure then—for the comparison, for the envy, for the injury. When the soul is dried out and thirsty, when the body is suffering, compassion becomes water.

CHAPTER EIGHT

FROST WARNING

On Setbacks

Illness is the doctor to whom we pay most heed; to kindness,
to knowledge, we make promise only; pain we obey.
— Marcel Proust

Last spring, I put my lemon tree sapling out on the back deck. I'd been keeping it alive inside all winter, in the only window that had an ounce of direct sun. It limped along under that window, desperately clinging to every bit of sunlight. By the time the weather warmed enough that it would survive, the tiny leaves were beginning to yellow. Within a day or two, the green returned to the sapling, and it grew well for a few weeks. I checked it daily. Every few days, a little green sprouting weed would pop up from the surface soil of the planter. I'm not sure exactly how those unwanted weedy shoots got to the planter, but they were tenacious and quick-growing. I plucked them out immediately to protect that little lemon tree.

While I was gone for a week on vacation, I neglected to

mention the care of the plants to the friend who housesat for us. She didn't notice the sapling resting in the small ceramic planter on the back porch. When I returned a week later, weeds had reached up and around the small stem, threatening to strangle it. I rescued my lemon tree just in time, and then I moved it to the small deck outside my bedroom and patted myself on the back for that save.

A few days later when I went to check on it, I was shocked to find that a squirrel had dug in the pot, uprooted the tree, and gnawed the tender top green leaves from it so that only a stem remained. I had grown that tree from a seed. The sense of satisfaction I took from sprouting the seed on a wet paper towel and growing it to this point was notable. The loss of that sapling felt like a tragedy. That small plant gave me next to nothing except proof that I could grow something and keep it alive, finally—and then the squirrels came and took me down a notch.

I left the stub there in the soil for a week, or maybe two. I hoped perhaps it might rise from the ashes, but not so. The hardest loss in my garden that spring was tossing out the remains of my lemon tree. It was hard to let go of that plant after sinking so much time and energy into it.

❖❖❖❖❖❖❖❖

> *i thank You God for most this amazing*
> *day: for the leaping greenly spirits of trees*

and a blue true dream of sky; and for everything
which is natural which is infinite which is yes

—e. e. cummings

MY MOTHER HAS A TALENT for growing roses. She knows the intricacies of several varieties that work best in Southern Ohio, there in the Miami Valley. She knows the hardiness of the thorny bushes. She knows when to pinch off the spent buds and when to prune back hard. She knows just how much they can bear of our strange, uneven winter seasons with their fluctuations. Cincinnati is situated in Planting Zone Six, Midwestern, and yet so close to the border of Kentucky it sometimes feels more Southern than Midwest. Across the river, the planting zone shifts as the climate warms just a little. We plan for Zone Six in either case because a cold snap or an early frost will shock the roses—perhaps enough to kill them, depending on the variety.

My mother would get alerts of frost warnings from the news or from neighbors and run to cover the bushes with blankets or trash bags, whatever we had on hand. But sometimes the frost came without warning. If the frost didn't kill the bushes, my mother would nurse them back to health, but it took time. Sometimes the damage would show up even the following spring. The rose bushes would limp along through the frost, the thaw, and the rain. They would produce smaller buds, they would be faded in color, they would succumb to insects. She would nurture the bush until she knew whether it was going to come back or not. She was always optimistic about it.

One spring, I got a phone call that my mother was in the hospital. She had not been feeling well the previous week and was finally persuaded by friends and family to go to the walk-in clinic. They admitted her because of her symptoms, her age, and her heart attack the year before. The heart attack had given some early warnings, so thankfully it was mild and treated quickly. In the months following it, she had no further heart trouble and was making good strides toward returning to her previous health level.

This most recent illness, however, escalated quickly from what she thought was the flu to colitis, to renal failure, and finally to the diagnosis of a rare blood disorder—all within the span of a few days. It was near the end of the week when the doctors finally were able to name her illness. It was called HUS, Hemolytic Uremic Syndrome. With this disease, which is a kind of autoimmune disorder and often a complication of an e-coli infection, the platelets of the blood go awry and begin to clot in all the wrong places. If not treated immediately, with a procedure similar to dialysis that filters the platelets out and replaces them with donor platelets, the patient will die quickly. My mother was in the hospital for twenty-one days and endured seventeen sessions of the three-hour treatments during that time. It saved her life.

The disease is one thing, the treatment another, but the

recovery from both is a story unto itself. We were told that for every one day in the hospital, she should expect a week of recovery at home, and because of my mother's age, it might take even longer. Before the illness, she was dancing once or twice a week with her clogging group for a couple of hours at a time. She was taking banjo lessons. She was working as a family therapist and a mediator, offering trainings and workshops, all while keeping the fabric of our extended family together.

The disease took her by surprise. She could not have planned for it. The recovery took her by surprise as well—emotionally, spiritually, and physically. Her days were roller coaster-like, with rising and falling emotions, healing rates, and energy levels. She found that the only way to work through the illness and the recovery was to take it a moment at a time. In those moments, she experienced both hope and fear in equal measure. Coming close to death has that effect.

❉❉❉❉❉❉❉❉❉

The wish for healing has always been half of health.
—Lucius Annaeus Seneca

A FRIEND OF MINE DIED OF CANCER before she was fifty. She'd always been fit, and to my knowledge, she tried to eat as healthfully as possible. The onset of this cancer seemed to come from nowhere. The diagnosis was traumatic, the treatment terrible; the recovery was uneven and ultimately unsuccessful. Once, in a tender moment, she confessed her anger toward her body. She said she felt her body was attacking her with the cancer, and yet, at the same time, she felt that her body had abandoned her. In that moment there was nothing I could think to say. What could I possibly say to a friend who is dying?

The best advice I ever received about being in relationship with someone who is suffering is that I should walk alongside—not run ahead, calling them to catch up, to keep their hopes high, to just "do it!" Neither should one lag behind, slowing their pace, encouraging them to look at the birds of the sky and the grass of the fields. So, in those conversations, I try to listen and be present. I want to argue, I want to cajole, I want to try to encourage that friend to fight, because that is what I want. It is what I need. In this case, her garden was dying, and there was nothing any of us could do about that. All I could do was take in her words, look into her eyes—still bright and living—and pay attention.

The notion of the body turning against one feels familiar to me, at least in some small measure. Beginning in my thirties, I would wake up in the morning feeling as though I had just run a marathon—muscles aching, fatigue draped over my head like a heavy blanket no matter how much sleep I got. My family doctor checked my thyroid for months, sticking the dreaded needle into my elusive veins and drawing out what I hoped would lead to some answers. The thyroid tests came back inconclusive each time. My doctor suggested perhaps I was suffering from a condition called fibromyalgia, a little-understood autoimmune disorder. The pain points, the stiffness, the fog that seemed to follow me throughout the day all gave these indications. Because the condition, even now, has been met with some skepticism, I mentally tucked the diagnosis into my purse and forgot about it. There was no medication to take, no real cure for the condition, no exact parameters for how to alleviate the symptoms except the warning that flare-ups are often triggered by stress.

Parenting and working freelance means that stress is a constant companion. The pain told me this in no uncertain terms. There were very good days, sometimes weeks or months, in which I felt no pain symptoms, but the fatigue and fog persisted with a strange continuity until I began to think this was just my new normal. I accepted the fog and the fatigue. On mornings when I woke with the hallmark pain, I moved like an eighty-year-old version of myself, and I cursed this body for the persistent aches, the frequent fog, the relentless fatigue.

It would make a good story to be able to say that I overcame the fibromyalgia, that the symptoms stopped, and that there was some miracle cure—food, water, medication, something that led to a miraculous return to health. But I can't, because it hasn't. Managing my stress has been a good treatment, paying attention to the pain has been a good treatment, changing some eating or exercise habits has been a good treatment, getting more information on the condition has been a good treatment, but nothing has cured it.

On bad mornings, I feel angry and worn down. I feel betrayed by this garden I have tried so hard to nurture. On bad days, I want to lie down and give up. I am convinced in those moments that this is all in my head, or perhaps it's something in my drinking water, or my occasional indulgence in doughnuts or dark chocolate. I want there to be a real, concrete cure, and I'm angry that despite having tried the cleanses, the supplements, the workout routines, the dietary changes that are touted with great fervor all around me, I am still in pain and drown in fatigue more often than I care to admit.

Sometimes there is no cure—the symptoms are chronic, but not fatal—and this is a strange place to live day after day. It is here, in good moments, and after a number of years to work out the mental gymnastics around this chronic illness, that I come back to the body as a "first child" concept. How would I care for a child with a chronic but not fatal illness? I imagine the moments of despair and hopelessness would be numerous. I imagine anger would rise, and would be, of course, justified. I imagine helplessness would sometimes feel like the ocean, with me a poor swimmer. And in between, or perhaps underneath, shoring it all up would be this foundation of care and love. I hope that is the foundation upon which I would build the relationship with that child, and I hope it is the foundation upon which I now build the relationship with this body with all its aches and pains. It is a challenge, my intentions are good, and I often fail. God bless the good intentions.

❦❦❦❦❦❦❦

The root of joy is gratefulness. . . It is not joy that makes us grateful; it is gratitude that makes us joyful.
—David Steindl-Rast

IF I CANNOT PLAN for every occurrence on the road to health, and I know there will be times during which I hit these patches of trouble, pain, difficulty—what then? I feel as though I hit these potholes in the road to wellness daily, sometimes hourly. When the frost comes without warning, how do we rise to the occasion? Apart from becoming informed, and seeking guidance from knowledgeable professionals and "walk alongside" companions in the journey, I'm convinced there is no other way to handle this except to take it one moment at a time, one decision at a time, one prayer at a time.

If there is a comfort I can cultivate, it begins in the good moments, healthy times, the straight-and-narrow days. It is twofold—prayer and gratitude. Prayer is as close as I might come to keeping the plants in this garden strong and well-watered while the good weather holds. Prayer builds solid root systems that run deep in the soil, systems that help to protect this garden at a level I cannot see on a daily basis. I know this communication with the divine Creator has an effect there under the ground—but it is quiet, foundational, and long building. Prayer is not a genie in a bottle waiting to grant my wishes, though in moments, I act as though it is. Prayer is slow, steady, rising the way incense perfumes the air or heavy the way rain waters the soil.

When I slow down a moment, open myself to this communication, and build this relationship with my Creator, and when I put myself back into right relationship with Him, I acknowledge the wonder of His creation, including this body I've been given. In this acknowledgment, whether weekly, daily, or hourly, I find I have a choice to make. Am I willing to be grateful for this garden here and now, come what may? Some days, some moments, I arrive at this easily, sounding out the simple yes that means I agree to these terms and conditions. But mostly I resist. I wish for the genie in the bottle, the better energy or freedom from pain and discomfort.

Or else I am likely to make a caveat—to myself, my friends, or anyone who will listen—"I'm grateful but . . . [insert complaint here]." Choosing gratitude means I accept myself as a beautiful gift rather than moving to discontent, comparison, or complaint. Building up prayer and gratitude when things are relatively smooth helps the "thank you" to roll more easily from my lips. In doing so, I hope I am more likely to turn to prayer and gratitude when the frost comes— with or without warning. Perhaps it is enough to carry me through. Gratitude builds and fortifies and keeps me open-hearted. It's hard to imagine what else builds my emotional immune system like this echinacea of the spirit.

Plant gratitude, tend it well, watch it bloom, and trust that even in the direst of circumstances, it will make a difference. It may not cure us, but given the proper care, the support of people who can walk alongside, and traveling companions who shore us up, it may yet carry us through.

CHAPTER NINE

THE STUMBLING RUNNER

On Exercise

The exercise of the body aims at the well-being of the body, because when it is healthy it helps man's spiritual condition. Similarly, man's spiritual well-being has consequences for the body.

—Metropolitan Hierotheos of Nafpaktos

Here's something beautiful. The human skeleton at birth is composed of 270 bones, which number decreases to 206 bones by adulthood after some bones have fused together. There are about 640 muscles in the human body, each with its own function, with insertion points either at a bone, a joint, or another muscle. The muscles work in groups—pushing, pulling, tensing and releasing.

There is a dance that happens throughout the human body when we move. The effort it takes our bones and muscles, working in concert, to turn the head or lift the hand is remarkable. Don't even get me started on the complexity of the brain impulses that order this movement, the nerves that carry out the orders, or the blood and oxygen that supply the whole system. We are designed to move, designed to lift and skip and reach. If everything is in good working order, we don't have to think about it all that much. We are a miracle, you know.

Once, while vacuuming, I threw my back out. I felt a twinge, and then a shooting pain ran down either side of my lower spine deep into my hips. I could not move. I had four small children, and it was the middle of the day. I made my way to the floor, instructed my daughter to turn off the vacuum cleaner and then give me the phone. When I told my husband I needed him to leave his meeting and come home, *right now*, he was confused. I'd never had a complaint about my back in my life. I was still awfully young for back trouble, and there was no immediate cause apart from vacuuming. When he came home and saw me weeping on the family room carpet, he remembered his own back issue and the pain he had encountered with it. He got the kids in line and me to the doctor.

There was no obvious physical reason for my back to go out—no injury, no inherent trouble with the spine or congenital defect as there is in my husband's case (he has spondylolisthesis, which is a slipping of the vertebrae). I was home full time then, working out as often as I could, but not eating or sleeping as well as I ought to have been. Still, I was in relatively decent shape for my tender mid-to-late thirties. The best my doctor could offer is that in addition to carrying children around and bending over picking things up off the ground all day, I was stressed out, and most likely I carried that stress in my lower back. I was parenting and vacuuming and worried, and one thing led to another until the twinge and pain came along to shut things down. After a massage, a lot of Advil, and some rest, my back pain finally subsided.

Pain is a signal. My body was telling me something. *Slow down. Pay attention. Breathe.* Overly tight muscles cannot do what they're made to do. When overly tight muscles are limited, restricted, and stiff, the muscles around those areas tend to try to pitch in and take up the slack. In truth, I'd felt twinges before—tiny spasms of pain, here and there. Weak signal flares telling me there was pain ahead. But I'd ignored them and kept going until at last the muscles took the action to reboot.

All things work together for the good. When one part of the body is suffering, other areas will rally to help support that part. Weak core muscles will gain some support from the lower back. They kick in to keep us upright even in the shadow of that core weakness. Over time those muscles, doing their job and that of the core, will begin to grow overworked, and then before you know it you're lying on the shag carpet, weeping in pain while your six-month-old son throws plastic blocks at your head from his bouncy chair.

What crystallizes for me in those moments leans less toward an appreciation for the miracle of this body and more toward regret for not caring well enough for it. Those small pains are reminders of my time spent so far on earth in concert with my relationship to gravity—and they have something important to tell me about the condition of this garden. They become like the small child pulling at my pant leg, repeating my name over and over while I'm on the phone. I know he needs something, but I'm already busy doing other things, so I hold the request at bay as long as I can.

I realize, in retrospect, that the best way to address those nagging reminders is to engage them, to pay attention in the moment. The persistent twinge pains are best given the prescription of movement with purpose and intention. By moving in the right way, at the right time, and in the right amount, I can begin to find ways to restore a full range of motion—but I have to get off the phone, pay attention, and listen first.

❧❦❧❦❧❦❧❦

> *Therefore I run thus: not with uncertainty. Thus I fight: not as one who beats the air. But I discipline my body and bring it into subjection, lest, when I have preached to others, I myself should become disqualified. (1 Cor. 9:26–27)*

MY BEST MEMORY OF GOING FOR A RUN is the time my athletically inclined sister suggested we head out and hit the pavement. It was a fine spring day, and we were both young, single, and relatively healthy. We warmed up, stretched, took some good cleansing breaths of that polluted Chicago air, and started out slow.

She had been running regularly, but this was new for me. I managed to avoid running at all costs, preferring instead to lift weights or do flexibility training when I worked out. We got about a block in, and I draped myself over a mailbox, frantically panting and waving her to go on and leave me behind. It probably didn't help that in those days I was smoking about half a pack of cigarettes a day. Even putting aside my compromised lung capacity at that time, I never cared for running. It was clear to me from a young age that running was not my thing.

I know a few things about myself as a runner. First, I know that my basic physiology doesn't lend itself well to this particular kind of exercise. I know now, after having surgery to repair that torn ligament in my knee, that my body mechanics don't mesh with hard impact on my joints. It's just the way I'm put together. Second, I know that I don't have to run if I don't want to; there are other ways to meet my fitness needs. So unless I am being chased by a bear or trying to catch a plane, I'm not going to run.

MY OLD INCLINATION toward comparison leaks in here too. I think about my friend Sarah and the fact that she has grown the most beautiful lavender I have seen in a home garden. The smell of the leaves, the brilliance of the bloom—it's remarkable. I think of my mother's gardening—her roses come to mind. When I think of abundant herb gardens, I remember my friend Jane and her incredible skills as a gardener.

It's a natural impulse to look at our friends' and family's and neighbors' gardens to see what they're growing, to see what blooms there, and to spot the beauty therein. If I'm in a good place with life, I'll simply appreciate that beauty; I'll thank God for the beauty, the friendships, the family, the stuff that grows and gives. If I'm not, I get out that measuring tape and find myself lacking.

Over the years, I have discovered that I do have some small talent for growing a weird mix of rosemary and sunflowers. I discovered the ability to grow giant sunflowers by accident. I let the kids pick out a pack of seeds from the store, and we buried them in our meager garden in a rush when we got home, because kid momentum is like that—do this, do it now, and then on to the next interesting thing. We forgot all about the sunflowers for a long time. The day they shot up outside the window of my kitchen, I felt like Jack witnessing his beanstalk rising up into the clouds.

The rosemary was a trial-and-error choice, an impulse buy that filled a spot in our yard in Tennessee. The other plants I chose that day died quickly, but the rosemary bush widened its branches and muscled through the whole space, filling it. I would brush up against that bush when walking from the garage to the back door, and the oils would linger on my hands and jeans. The more the bushes grew, despite my shortcomings, the prouder and more capable I felt to continue to try to grow things.

It's an odd grouping on my growable plants list, but it works, and it's encouraging. It makes me more inclined to try new things, and I like these plants. I like what they stand for—rosemary for remembrance, and sunflowers in all their awkward and open-faced brilliance. When I hit on the thing that works, I try to take note of it. I start there and then build the plants that fit along with it—the ground covering, the shrubs at the end points, the perennials that come in the spring, the mulch that cushions and protects.

It's a mistake to think that if I am unable to grow what my mom or my friends grow, I am unable to grow anything at all. I was just working with the wrong plants for my soil at that time. Ultimately, I need to keep my eyes on my own garden. I had to find my thing. Where exercise is concerned, if I give up trying anything physical because of my stumbling while running, I'm at a profound loss.

When the tool is blunted, it hinders the artist, no matter how quick and skillful he may be. . . . A man should keep to right judgment in all things so that he will not stumble.
—Elders Barsanuphius and John

"YOU SHOULD COME. IT'S FUN!" she said, and I believed her. My friend Carol was doing a hip-hop tribal dance cardio kind of class, and I was reluctant to try it. I do not care for jumping, and this seemed to include a lot of jumping. The bulk of my experience of dance came in high school when I started sneaking into punk rock clubs. Slam dancing was the simplest and most rudimentary form of dancing I was able to master. In my case, dancing meant lurching around in a crowded room of sweaty peers and just bumping into one another randomly. Story of my life. I already did this in the hallways at school all the time, albeit unintentionally, so it turns out I was good at that.

I went to the class, but I did not *want* to go to the class. The cardio workout was coordinated and timed, high-energy music pumped from the sound system, and the instructor barked out enthusiastic cues. I kept up as best I could, appreciating at the very least that I was seeing a diversity of bodies around me; mostly women but all shapes, sizes, and shades. It was a beautiful sight. When I think about that class, this diversity is what I remember best. What kept me from going back was my lack of confidence and the fact that I just didn't care much for the jumping around to loud music. I think I'm getting old. Don't tell anybody.

Another friend persuaded me to attend a belly-dancing class. I enjoyed that, especially the part when we tied brightly colored, chiming chain-laden scarves around our hips and shook. I was immediately seven years old again playing dress-up. I felt so happy in that moment—but it was short-lived. In the end, the draw was not quite compelling enough to keep me coming back. Life got in the way. Dress-up was the first to get the axe in my schedule, and that's a terrible admission. Dress-up ought to get more airtime.

My sister-in-law insists that I need to try her boot-camp workout. They meet at six am three times a week. They sweat a lot by flipping tractor tires through a parking lot. They have an instructor yell at them like a drill sergeant. They run laps and speed sprints. I think it sounds awful, but she swears by it. She tells me she tears herself out of bed every time, and every morning she dreads it and makes excuses not to go, but once she's there, she's glad to be there. She's engaged and interested. She feels alive.

And it occurs to me that I often have these same feelings when faced with getting up and out of the house to attend Liturgy. As much as I love it when I am there, and feel as though it fuels me until I return again, my warm bed on Sunday morning is appealing. French toast or waffles when

I rise is appealing. The hot cup of coffee and a good book in the comfy chair near the window is appealing. I forget in those appealing moments about the lasting effects of Liturgy, how it unwinds me, slows me down, engages my mind in such a way that I am able to find that descent into the depths of my heart. Liturgy sorts me out. I need that, and often I do not remember this until I drag myself out of the house and into the church.

Through my trying and stumbling and keeping at it, I have discovered that I like strength training. Free weights or machines, doesn't matter. I like to pump iron, and my body responds well to it. I also know that I enjoy flexibility training. I can take a strength or flexibility class that runs an hour or longer, and it feels as though no time has passed—unlike spending time on the treadmill, or cardio classes that seem to me as though they will never end. When I reach that place in exercise where I can forget myself, leave behind the clock and the pace, and just breathe into and focus on whatever I am doing at the moment, I know I have found my exercise "thing."

My sister's thing is running; my friend Carol's thing is hip-hop dancing. My thing is stretching, deep breathing, slow and controlled. My thing is setting weight stacks and pressing into, pushing out of, lifting or lowering the heavy load. In a way, it's a good mirror for the spiritual life—engaging the struggle, breathing into the discomfort of this present moment. Just showing up is half of it. Once there, it sorts me.

And while I'm not keen on flipping tractor tires or having someone bark orders behind me, there are elements of my exercise thing that sort me the way my sister-in-law gets sorted by boot camp, the way Liturgy sorts me in my spiritual life. I procrastinate, I beg off, I reason with myself, but if I show up, I see and feel how true it is. I feel it in my bones and muscles. I feel it in my spirit, in my step, in my soul.

When you find this sorting, you recognize it like a long-lost friend, like a hymn you used to know. When you find it, hold onto it. Write it down so you remember. When you find your thing, you need to protect it, guard that time to build this foundation of the garden. This is the plant that blooms despite your worst efforts. This is the act that is self-forgetting so that time moves so quickly you are in awe when it is over, and perhaps too, you are a little bit sad it is done for the day.

I know that when I do it right and do it well, physically, my body takes notice. My soul takes notice. My mood improves. My step is lighter. Sometimes the muscles tell me with delayed soreness, but it's that nice reminder that I have worked hard, not the pain of the back gone out from the daily stress of things. It's that lactic acid that had been languishing in the muscle fibers at last set loose. It's an indication that strength is coming, that perseverance is requested, and rest is also required to rebuild those muscles. I am engaged and interested. I feel energized. I feel alive.

Find your thing, whether it's belly dancing, strength training, stretching, or boot camp. And then branch out— let the energy and confidence bring you outside your comfort zone once in a while, the way Liturgy leads us more deeply into prayer, calling us to attend, not just that Sunday morning but daily, hourly, praying without ceasing. When you find your thing, do it. See how you feel. See how it changes the picture over time. See how it sorts the body—with time and patience, with consistency and care, as Liturgy sorts the spirit, as seasons sort the garden.

CHAPTER TEN

COMFORTABLY NUMB

On Avoidance

Let nothing perturb you, nothing frighten you. All things
pass. God does not change. Patience achieves everything.
—Teresa of Ávila

There were only a few patches of our yard on Manor Street that got adequate sun. The mulberry trees on the property blocked out the sun on the half lot next to the house. That lot is what sold us on the house. We thought it would be perfect for our growing family. Coming across an affordable house with a little green space in Chicago was a real find, but that green space was all weedy ground cover when the spring came. Apart from two spots in the front near the sidewalk, it was all ground cover, clover, or creeping myrtle.

The two sunny spots were filled with overgrown plantings of day lilies. When I was a kid, I saw lilies like this in my neighbor's yard. We called them tiger lilies, and my best friend, Margaret, and I would pick them and play Peter Pan by her garage. She always got to be Tiger Lily because they were her flowers, and it was her yard. Fair enough.

I didn't like the day lilies in our yard when they came up that first spring. The stand of flowers was cramped, and they competed for the small area, producing only a few blooms to the widening mass of green leaves. The blooms that did appear were spilling out from their small circle of light and beginning to sag outward. Friends advised me on the proper way to thin the lilies, but between small children running around and sleep deprivation, I didn't have the time or energy to devote to digging to the roots and pulling up the entire clump to divide and then replant.

In a moment of desperation and exasperation, I took out the lawn mower near the end of that spring and ran them all down. Then I mowed the shady ground cover too. For the rest of that season, I mowed the area instead of tending it. It felt great. I had a Zen-like appreciation for the clean look of it, but I knew it wouldn't last. Mowing the lilies would only give me a short period of relief. There would be deep digging ahead in the spring once again if I didn't take the time to thin the lilies, retill the lawn, and resow the grass. I would never get the landscape to look or feel the way I hoped by just mowing it down.

Even now, when faced with a hard process of change, I notice this tendency to just cut my losses and take the quick and simple route. I think to myself, when faced with making new, difficult health choices—*Am I just mowing the lilies here?* Sometimes the answer is yes, and yet sometimes the yes is necessary. Mowing the lilies allows me to clear the field long enough to figure out what I'd rather see there. It's a learning process, a clearing process—but a temporary measure, at best.

⁂

SOMETIMES I CONFUSE my pain and my fatigue. When I am walking or lifting and the nagging comes in my lower back, my calves, my arms, I question it. I knew it was coming. It's not surprising. I think to myself, *Here's my stopping point* or *Here's my push-through point.* Some days I push through, some days I stop.

Fatigue is the expected heat we feel in the muscle when we perform an action over and over. Fatigue in the muscle tells us we're reaching a decision time, and we'd best prepare for that. But pain tells us to stop—right now. The old phrase, "no pain, no gain," has never been valid for the general population. I suppose if I were a professional athlete, it might be hard to avoid pain in the competition, but in training and for the general population, I never want to elicit this response in the body. I work hard to avoid it.

I forget in the middle of the process that what I want is to be able to move better, to live stronger and longer. I starve my muscles. I starve my spirit. I starve my belly. I think, mistakenly, that this is the path forward, because that's the message I seem to take in day after day. Sacrifice becomes a conflicted notion. Pain equals gain. It's a lie—and it's a lie that can lead to injury. On the other hand, I sometimes swing too far in the other direction—toward apathy, toward becoming numb. The couch is comfortable. The distractions are plentiful. It's easy to mow the lilies. It's easier than digging and separating and replanting.

The remembrance of pain can be a strong influencer as well. Remembered injuries are stored in our muscles. We create new pathways in the brain to avoid that injury again. It's an easy maneuver to sideline myself in the name of care. Becoming engaged in the world, trying again, working a little harder—these actions can be terrifying, so I use things to medicate me when the remembered pain of injuries or the fear of failure crops up. Some people medicate with status, some with sex, some with focus on other transient and worldly things. Food tends to be a frequent medication for me, but avoidance by means of making myself too busy or too distracted works too.

I tell myself it's natural to medicate when we feel pain, to use avoidance when we are afraid, and of course, it is. Avoidance and medication can feel self-protective. I confuse the medication with rest. This is where I make a long slide into apathy or avoidance. But rest, in its best form, when the fatigue is real, when the pain is real and not imagined, is nurturing and necessary. There is a gift in rest.

Farmers will leave fields fallow for seasons to give the soil a chance to regenerate. This is not avoidance, but rather a kind of active rest. It is done with intention, planning, and care, keeping in mind the whole of the growing season. It's a short-term method to support the long-term goal—a long and fruitful life for the land. Rest is a dynamic part of the process of taking care of this garden. Still, the idea that it is all right to rest gets lost in the jumble of my active life—parenting and schoolwork, job responsibilities, relationships, lawn care. Who has time for the luxury of rest?

I recognize that becoming numb and seeking to medicate the stress is not the same thing as seeking this active rest. Watching an episode or two of a television show is fine, perhaps. Watching an entire season in a day because I'm overwhelmed with daily life is avoidance. This avoidance becomes destructive when it tears me down rather than building me up. Mowing the lilies won't solve it, but neither will letting them grow untended and neglected.

For just as a runner is obstructed and weighed down by clothing, so too is the intellect by anxious thoughts.
—St. Evagrios the Solitary

ST. EVAGRIOS THE SOLITARY did me a favor this morning. I've been slogging through a pile of required reading for a project all month, but sometimes I'd rather binge-watch a season of *Hell's Kitchen* instead. I'll confess that sometimes I actually *do* binge-watch seasons of *Hell's Kitchen* instead. It is a way to avoid the hard work of whatever the text is likely to confront as I read it. I question myself as I revert to just one more episode, just one more season. What am I avoiding? What am I neglecting? Why am I so tired and burned out?

In time, I drag myself back around to that pile of required reading, and I fight the guilt of the lost time. I work to get back on track as though the required reading were a strict diet of tree bark and bitter vegetables, and I had spent the day before eating metaphorical Twinkies and Ho-Hos. But I am back to my regular working diet now. Sitting with butt in chair and pondering words from the required reading I have laid aside. It's a new day, free of Gordon Ramsey and his temperamental outbursts, filled instead with St. Eva-grios the Solitary telling me things that have been gathered in the *Philokalia* by St. Nikodemos of the Holy Mountain.

I celebrate a little because I am finally past the introduction. If you've read it, you know what I mean. The *Philokalia* can be thick and heady. It can be difficult to chew, sticking to my teeth if not my brain. The introduction alone was enough to make me want to spit it out, though I know that in the savoring of it, in the rumination, the taste is sweet, the benefits are vast. But now I am finally entering into the nitty gritty, words written centuries ago by the Church

Fathers, monastics, ascetics, saints. This chapter by St. Evagrios is numbered—one, two, three—like Proverbs, like stereo instructions, like recipes.

After three, maybe four numbered instructions for living well, for listening in, for following God, I am distracted and brain numb. I am ready for either a snack or a run in the park—but probably a snack, because I don't run. I stare at the pattern of the carpet, hoping I gleaned something important in that short spurt of reading deep words from Church Fathers. I am hoping the words crawled into my ailing soul and made a home there. I am hoping that by osmosis I will somehow be able to access those words later, because now I just want a snack or a run—but probably a snack. I am feeling guilty then. I would much rather be scanning social media or reading something fluffy and fun. I would much rather walk than run, lift light and count it as all good.

In the midst of my distraction and guilt, St. Evagrios hits me with a sweet gem about running and being weighted down. He hits me with reminders about my anxiety, my mind always working. I *am* anxious—and I did not realize it until just this moment. And that anxiety does feel heavy—like walking or running with winter clothes on after having a swim in them. Rather than going home and taking off those wet and frozen anxious thoughts, I am seeking shelter in doorways or in the temporary heat lamps at bus stops. It feels good in the moment, but it won't last long. What I need is to get someplace safe and warm and take off those cold, wet clothes.

When St. Evagrios speaks of the intellect, he is referring to the *nous,* which indicates something more along the lines of the heart, the lens with which we see the world around us and the language we use to communicate with the One who made us. When the nous is cloudy or obscured, I am out of touch with myself and with my Creator. I'm misunderstanding, I'm misled, I'm out of sync, tired and overwrought, slogging along the daily run of life wearing that heavy, wet winter coat. The anxiety, the guilt, the avoidance are exhausting—they will wear us down, they will bring us to the brink.

* * *

Therefore we also, since we are surrounded by so great a cloud of witnesses, let us lay aside every weight, and the sin which so easily ensnares us, and let us run with endurance the race that is set before us, looking unto Jesus, the author and finisher of our faith, who for the joy that was set before Him endured the cross, despising the shame, and has sat down at the right hand of the throne of God. For consider Him who endured such hostility from sinners against Himself, lest you become weary and discouraged in your souls. (Heb. 12:1–3)

I CAN ALWAYS TELL when I'm on the verge of a head cold. There are subtle warnings—the tightening throat, the mild congestion, the headache. The cold usually comes on the heels of my children or husband having been sick. I know I'm next in line for it, but I like to think I mentally hold it all together until the timing is right. When I'm on the verge of illness, I actually catch myself thinking, "I cannot afford to be sick yet, but after such and such date, I can take time off."

Then, like clockwork, right after the deadlines are met and I've cleared the metaphorical busy-making forest, I wake up in the full throes of the cold. I find it lingers in my head and chest a long time as I glide back into busy seasons. It feels like a game I play with my body, a kind of strange carrot-on-a-stick technique to get me from point A to point B. I'm cheering myself along, like the crowd that lines the route for a long-distance runner. Just one more lap, just one more mile running at full speed, and finally, I collapse at the finish line. I rest for a short time, and then I see the next race starting up ahead. There is no real time for resting.

Marathon racers don't function like this. They don't simply wake up one day and run races. They train in a holistic way—strength work, short runs that are gradually lengthened, planning their races so they are spaced out well enough to support their goals. They watch their food intake. They make notes about their running time, their flexibility training, and their sleep; they take days off—they rest. We are metaphorical marathon runners, all of us, but we don't always think to train like them. What we ought to work toward is endurance.

Marathon training as it applies to the lifelong task of tending the garden means that while I may go through periods of fallow time, let us say, I also pay attention to the tilling, the planting, the harvest. I will have seasons during which the training is exact and the pacing is steady. I will have times during which the air turns cold or stormy, and I'll have to endure the discomfort of that run. And I will have times in which I should allow myself to rest, a prescribed and supportive rest, to let the muscles adapt and rebuild. Rest is natural and necessary. Pushing myself until rest is mandated by my body collapsing in defeat is ultimately harmful.

When I allow this rest and plan for it, embrace it, take hold of it, the body can rebuild and regroup. But it's important for me to be able to recognize the difference between fallow times and avoidance. It's evident in the heart and spirit. Being worn down, being tired, being utterly exhausted after parenting or working or just the ongoing business of living life requires those seasons of rest. Just getting enough sleep on a given night does amazing repair work on the body, and in turn, the spirit. In order to run the long race, rest is a necessary ingredient. I know this somewhere inside. I keep that information stored in the closets of my brain.

Working until I collapse is another thing altogether. This is neglect. This is avoiding the body signals that tell me to stop and rest. Just as pain is the body's way of signaling injury, exhaustion signals a need to slow down, to pay attention, and to rest. I have to open up those closets and relearn the signals, learn to read the memos I get from the body that tell me it's time to rest, pay attention so that I can honor them long before I encounter the utter exhaustion and depletion.

It's a risk to stop what we're doing and spend the day relaxing, or to stop working a little early and go to bed at a decent hour. I have this odd notion that just one more hour of work will push everything to the next, better level, but it comes at a cost. It is in avoiding regular rest times that I may be more likely to medicate with other things. These false medications stem the exhaustion and stave off the torpor that creeps into my overworked brain and body.

Sleep and choosing to rest ought to have equal footing with eating and exercise where health is concerned. When I honor those fallow seasons or even simple moments of rest, then the desire to medicate with avoidance *will* ease. I have to trust this. When I stop seeing rest as a commodity to be hoarded, I will begin to know it as a regular, justified, and lasting form of self-care. A short-term practice for long-term benefits, letting the garden rest long enough to let the soil regain its lost vitality, for the plants to reset and be restored. This holistic care of the garden, with seasons of feast and seasons of fallow, affords me opportunities for moments of rest and reset. I remind myself that this is, after all, a marathon, not a quick dash to the next, possibly better thing. Slow and steady finishes the race.

CHAPTER ELEVEN

SUSTENANCE

On Eating

Food for the body is not enough. There must be food for the soul.

—Dorothy Day

Grandma Doll's house was always full of people. Most of her twelve children still lived in Ohio when I was young, and all of them had children of their own. My family would drive up to Dayton from Cincinnati as often as we could to visit. There were usually kids running around the yard when we pulled up. The youngest of the cousins were inside, seated around the table with their parents, while the older cousins would congregate in the cool, dark basement to play board games or poker.

The walls of the basement were lined with shelves from floor to ceiling all around. The shelves were filled with the canning my grandmother would do every season from the vegetables she'd gather from her abundant garden. We always had green beans, corn, cucumbers, cherries, apples, rhubarb, and zucchini from the store in that basement.

Years later, after my grandfather died and my grandmother sold the house to move into a retirement home, my dad and his siblings cleared out their house. They tossed more jars of canned produce than they could count. She had kept up her gardening and canning and preserving long after most of the kids and grandkids moved further away. Having been raised in the Depression, her natural instinct was to store up. My dad's parents operated from a place of scarcity, the fear of not having enough. The feeling followed them through the lean times and informed their sense of food even in times of plenty. So until the end, she was lining those walls—*just in case*.

We did not have room for a vegetable garden at my house growing up, but my dad followed his mother's example and grew zucchini and tomatoes in a small strip of land alongside the building that housed his paint business in Hillsboro, Ohio. He'd drive an hour to work each way, sometimes staying the night in his lab there. He'd come home with his truck full of produce from that small patch garden. My mom took the bounty and canned the tomatoes for spaghetti sauce, the cucumbers became pickles, and the zucchini was baked into spiced bread with raisins or walnuts. The life of the garden showed up on the table all throughout my childhood. The fresh produce sustained us in lean times, as the garden had sustained my father's family.

When I was a child, I lived in the world of magical thinking. I could lie on the ground, there in the green grass
between my grandmother's garden and the small orchard
of fruit trees that bordered it, and stare at the sky without
the heavy weight of adult life on my shoulders yet. I'd find
shapes in the clouds. I'd think about the possibility of fairies
and elves living in the flowers. Thinking *what if* was a process
of magical thinking. What if I had wings? What if I could fly
into that blue sky? But even with my child mind, rooted in
a world of possibilities, I felt some phantom sense of scarcity
pressing in. That sense of scarcity hung on the air around
me, inherited from my grandparents or from my parents.
Perhaps I inhaled it without realizing it.

As I became an adult, the magical *what if* morphed slowly
into a reflection of my fears rather than my hopes. What if
the river floods? What if the crocuses don't come up in the
spring? What if I am not enough? It may be that this is just
a standard byproduct of growing up. It was the end of an era
when I let my "what ifs" change into a posture of fear rather
than curiosity. I try to remember when it was that I gave in
to those notions—when I placed ideas into jars, sealed and
static, lining the walls of me for *just in case*.

But asking "what if" can be a kind of courage too—if I
can challenge my old static ideas with this question, I can
return to curiosity. I become an intrepid scientist, positing
theories, striking out into the unknown. I want to ask ques-

tions. I want to stay curious, even when it feels risky. I want to leave behind that fearful place of scarcity, the part of me that stores up, and reins in, and worries about not having or being enough.

I see this scarcity thinking crop up in various places in my life, but nowhere near as often as when I consider what and how to eat. I find myself standing in the grocery store paralyzed with indecision. There are too many choices, too many ingredients, too many options, and each comes with baggage I have brought into the store with me. I have been building this fear for a long time, through many channels. I have had seeds of scarcity planted from childhood, heirloom seeds from past generations. How to eat well and still live with purpose and integrity, health and delight, is often a mystery to me, even now. I wish I felt confident enough to say aloud to my children, "Here is the perfect thing," but time and experience tell me otherwise. I worry about the seeds I am planting in my children's psyches where eating is concerned. I think about it a lot.

---

*Not that I speak in regard to need, for I have learned
in whatever state I am, to be content: I know how to be
abased, and I know how to abound. Everywhere and in all
things I have learned both to be full and to be hungry, both
to abound and to suffer need. I can do all things through
Christ who strengthens me. (Phil. 4:11–13)*

WHEN I BECAME A MOTHER for the first time, I read as many books as I could on parenting and the care of babies. Reading books when I'm anxious about something helps me feel more prepared for the task. In books, parenting looks easy—laid out in step-by-step, well-reasoned and researched directions. In practice, parenting is far more difficult. It is messy and haphazard, sometimes terrifying and yet always beautiful, even in the messy moments.

My daughter, my firstborn, taught me about the gap between good parenting theory and stark reality. I was careful about her diet, and mine, that first year of her life. I took some pride in being overly focused on our sugar intake and took it so far as to make her birthday cake that first year from a recipe I got from a crunchy-momma book. Instead of white sugar and flour, which I judged to be evil based on my reading, I used carrots, honey, whole-wheat flour, and raisins. The "cream cheese" frosting included no cream cheese at all and barely resembled frosting of any kind. I spent a great deal of time baking this healthy treat to celebrate her first birthday, all the while thinking about what a great precedent I was setting. I thought I was really winning at this parenting thing.

In theory, this cake was nutritionally perfect. In reality, it was awful. I mean it tasted terrible—so terrible my daughter wouldn't eat it. Once I tried it for myself, I didn't blame her. I sorted through the disappointment of what I considered a massive failure on my part. I have pictures of those "first cake" moments. You know those iconic photos—the baby sits by the cake happy, the baby digs her fingers into the cake happy, the baby stuffs her smiling face with gooey icing while parents laugh. In our photos, Riley looks at the cake with skepticism, digs her chubby fingers into the brown carrot mess with trepidation, shoves it into her mouth reluctantly, and then summarily spits it out. I have no photographic evidence of this next part of the event, but I'm pretty sure she then looked at me and shook her head at the utter disgrace of that first cake. To this day, she doesn't care much for carrot cake.

Over time I became disenchanted with the process of preparing, choosing, and eating delicious food. I thought everything I ate or prepared had to be a certain nutritional level, a certain color, a certain time of day. Cooking, buying groceries, and sitting down to eat became mixed up in the ongoing fight between what I wanted and what I thought I *ought* to eat based on magazine articles, and books I read, and stories I heard from friends. I had begun, almost without realizing it, to label food as "good" or "evil."

I was looking at my neighbors' plates, or the latest eating trends, or best-selling books, wondering which miracle food would cure my ills. Food had moved out of an experience of the family table, abundant, celebratory, and sustaining. What's worse was the feeling of judgment that washed over me as time wore on. The more extreme my mindset, the more judgmental and critical I became. It was an ugly practice, sustained by my long-time, well-cultivated fears.

I aim for middle ground now. But for a long time, middle ground seemed to be a place I flew past—like swings of the pendulum between the poles of "I buy only healthy foods" and "Ugh, I give up, let's eat this candy bar while hiding in the pantry." The swing toward judgment and the hyperfocus on "eating healthy" was just as bad as the apathy and depression that came on the other end, in what felt like my inability to "do it right." When operating from a place of scarcity or fear, it can feel as though there is no middle ground on which to land. It can feel like only ocean beneath me, murky and expansive.

Once, in the middle of a flight over the ocean of that elusive middle ground, I invited my friend Sarah and her family to dinner. I asked if they had any dietary restrictions I should keep in mind. "Nope," she said, "we are delishatarians. If it is delicious, we will eat it!" That idea clung to me. There's abundance in that idea. There is joy and celebration. When had I forgotten that food ought to be delicious? That it ought be savored and enjoyed? I know this represents a deep truth about food and eating, some truth I had laid aside along with that cloud-watching and magical thinking. Food is delicious. Food is blessing. This thought took root in me. It sticks to my brain in a way I cannot always grasp from meal to meal, but it clings to me still, and I'm thankful for it.

Negative judgment of myself, my food, my neighbor does nothing for me in the long run. It only taints the soil in which I grow. Judgment and guilt ruin the appetite, choking whatever I plant—the garden starves, and I starve. I recognize if I continue to hold on with each swing of the pendulum over middle ground that I have no idea how to choose well, no idea how to trust my instincts, or even what my instincts ought to be. Food becomes an enemy to be vanquished rather than a delishatarian exploration, a joyful experience—and I want this. Why wouldn't I want to choose joy over fear? Sustenance over scarcity?

❉❉❉❉❉❉❉❉❉❉

> *And as they were eating, Jesus took bread, blessed and broke it, and gave it to them and said, "Take, eat; this is My body." (Mark 14:22)*

WHEN, IN THE GOSPEL OF MARK, the author tells us that Jesus took the bread, blessed and broke it, the word used for *blessed* in the Greek is *eulogéo*, literally translated as "to speak well of" or "to confer what is beneficial." The food becomes blessed, becomes blessing. When I take food as blessing, it means I am reaching further into God's grace, accepting what is before me as a gift, with a measure of respect and wonder. In this way, I give thanks. In this way I nurture the garden without overwatering or allowing the soil to dry and crumble around the roots of the plants I mean to grow.

This is the basis for that delishatarian posture, putting food back into its proper place in my life. Whether I view food in that moment as fuel or medicine or sustenance, or all of it at once—food is blessing. It is celebratory and joyful, delicious and life-giving, no longer "good" or "bad" and not given the false power of moral labels. I glimpse this in a meal here or there, not always, but with some increasing regularity. It's hard work to untangle old messages and ideas. It's hard work to put aside my tendency to become judgmental or self-righteous where eating is concerned. Eyes on my own plate, eyes on the plates I put on my family table, eyes on my heart. Who's to judge?

When I choose to move food back into a place of blessing—with commitment and intention, supported by prayer, awareness, and good counseling—I can hope for deep shifts on every level. Clearing away that old growth in the area of eating and the attitude toward food means I am moving one step closer to appropriate care and love of the body as a way to respect the gift of this garden. Food becomes delicious again, eating becomes blessing, like water when the soil is dry, like the strong sun revealed after a long winter. When I choose to eat because I want to be nurtured, and because that food is delicious and supports my long-term sustainable health goals, I am back in right relationship. I aim to set goals for good health—body and soul—and then eat to support those goals. I aim to keep food and eating in their true place and find the blessing in each meal. I take time to taste each bite, to savor the flavor on my tongue, the blessing on my lips. Amen and amen.

❈❈❈❈❈❈❈❈❈

> *As the fathers have pointed out, bodies vary greatly in their need for food. One person needs little, another much to sustain his physical strength, each according to his capacity and habit.*
>
> —St. Gregory of Sinai

AFTER MY HUSBAND HAD CANCER in 1998, he became a vegetarian for a while. He wasn't following a doctor's prescription or a scientific study or magazine article. He just wanted to try it, to see how he felt by changing the way he viewed his eating. We did well for about a year. In some ways, it was easier for him than for me. I did not feel the pull toward vegetarianism, but I cooked the meals for him and our family, and I did what I could to support him in it.

In time, he came back to eating meat, but the trip down the vegetarian road offered him some good health benefits and expanded his understanding of the role food had taken in his life over the years. He was, in effect, resetting his thinking on food and eating by paying attention for a time.

By taking on a short-term challenge to reorient his eating habits, he was able to find some middle ground again. For him, it was an exploration, not a punishment or a cure-all for his condition.

When he let go of the vegetarian eating, he didn't consider it a failure in any respect. He was grateful for that time and then moved forward. I like that about him. He has a way of choosing the good, operating not out of scarcity but out of abundance. For my husband, life is meant to be savored and embraced. Meat was not "bad" when he was a vegetarian; it was just not supporting the health and lifestyle goals he'd set for that time.

Food is more than fuel—it is complicated and chemical, beautiful and functional, just as my body is more than machinery. If I treat my body as a garden, then food becomes sustenance for that garden. It acts in harmony with that garden. The root word of sustenance is "sustain." It comes from the Old French *sustenir* meaning "hold up, endure." What sustains me? What holds me up so that I can endure and greet the cycles of the seasons as they come?

I can tell when I am tempted to make the slide into that pendulum swing again, and into the disordered thinking that fuels that swinging, instead of keeping feet on middle ground. When I start to label food as "poison" when it isn't literally poison, it's a problem. When I start to demonize entire food groups although I have no medical reason to avoid them, that too is a problem. When I stop enjoying the tastes and textures of the meals I am eating, stop going out to restaurants with friends because of self-imposed restrictions, or feel the need to lecture others about what they eat, then I know I have an unhealthy relationship to food.

And it cuts me then, both ways—overly restrictive eating, even when it's leaning too far toward "healthy" or "clean" foods, or eating absently and without care. I cannot escape injury when I choose the pendulum between those two distant points. When my approach to eating moves out of sustenance and takes on an unearned reverence or fear, I know my thinking is disordered.

When setting and evaluating my ongoing, long-term goals for health, it may come to pass that I'll need to ease up in one area or another for a time. Sometimes a dietary change or restriction is warranted, as rest is warranted where exercise is concerned or watering is warranted when compassion is lacking. Eating well to support long-term health goals is not disordered, but just as prayer practices can vary according to needs and abilities, dietary changes will vary from person to person. Food might be medicine, but your prescription is probably different from mine.

What needs healing is my relationship to the food I'm eating. Healthy eating isn't about eating only foods I judge as "good" or healthful. It's about having a healthy relationship with all the foods I choose to eat. I leave the guilt, and judgment, and crazy-making labels behind so that I can see the middle ground again. Middle ground is sustainable, enduring. Middle ground is the safest place to land.

CHAPTER TWELVE

MAY DAY

On asking for help

We always need a coach, someone adept at the secrets of all sports to teach us obedience and the acquisition of knowledge.

—Metropolitan Hierotheos of Nafpaktos

My friend Jane is a gifted gardener. She's a natural at a number of things, but in this she truly excels. She has the Midas touch where plants are concerned. When we moved to our first house in Chicago, she was the one who broke the news to me that the trees in our yard were mulberries. She gave me some advice about how to clean up after them. She is the one who gasped when she saw that I'd mowed down my day lilies. She's a forgiving garden-loving friend.

Once at the start of our friendship, while we were at her house for dinner, she handed me a pair of small shears and sent me out to her herb garden to cut some fresh thyme. At that time, I had never seen or used fresh thyme, but I was embarrassed to mention this. So I puttered around the fragrant garden for a few minutes, just poking around, hoping for a sign, literally, to guide me. After a few minutes, Jane came out and asked if everything was all right. I had to confess that I had no idea what I was looking for, so she took a few minutes to give me a quick tour of the garden. She not only instructed me about the thyme but also showed me her fresh basil, rosemary, and tarragon plants.

What is striking to me about this memory is that in the moment I felt overwhelmed with the beauty of the place—the scent, the possibilities, the bounty of it all—and I also felt completely inadequate. Even with the small space afforded by the tiny yards in the city of Chicago, Jane was able to make this amazing garden flourish—beautiful and functional to boot. I am still in awe of the mad skills she shows in the area of gardening, and I am still ashamed that the first place I go with that memory is that feeling of comparison and inadequacy. Through the years of our friendship, I have promised myself time after time that I'm going to call her and have her share with me her ninja gardening techniques, but I don't follow through nearly enough. I know now how much trouble I might have saved myself if I had only reached out to her.

It's that lie of self-sufficiency I harbor deep inside. It's the strange message of "I ought to know this already" or "I ought to be further along by now." The trouble wasn't that I didn't know, but that I was unwilling to ask for help and unwilling to admit how little I knew. Pride keeps me from asking. I can read and research for days or months, but when push comes to plant, I need help. I need to set aside my pride because I need guides. I need support. This is not a failing.

❦❦❦❦❦❦❦

I will lift up my eyes to the hills—
From whence comes my help?
My help comes from the LORD,
Who made heaven and earth. (Ps. 121:1–2)

OUR HOUSE IN TENNESSEE is seated on eighteen acres—some wooded, some field. The realtor suggested we cut down the fields that were close to the house to keep the snakes away. *Snakes.* That was all I needed to hear to take his advice. Moving to the country was already a difficult transition; I didn't need fanged wildlife thrown into the mix.

So that first year we had the fields mowed down all the way to the tree line. We could see the expanse of the acreage. I felt suddenly vulnerable. The cleared fields were already browned and dying when we moved there, but I had no idea how much cover it had offered us, even in the middle of nowhere. The winter was long that year, the morning frost on the newly groomed fields was beautiful and temporary, melting away as the sun reached each sheared blade of grass left there.

The following year, when we felt more comfortable with

the land, we decided to let the fields grow again to see what the springtime offered. We had the mowers make a path through the fields on either side of the house so we could reach the woods more easily. That spring the field grew wide and tall, filling with wildflowers and butterflies. By the fall and early winter, the field threatened to take over the whole area, especially there along the edges of the woods, but it was not easily reachable for the mowers.

Dave decided to do what is called a "controlled burn." We were still relatively new to the area, and new to the country life, but the Internet is a magical place filled with all kinds of helpful information. Between that and the country living books we'd purchased when we moved there, we felt confident this was something we could pull off without too much trouble.

For a few hours, Dave burned the edges of the field, working his way slowly along the line of trees. Gray-black smoke curled up as I watched from the living room. My brother, nephew, and friend were in town that weekend, so I watched as they moved casually from one edge to the other, tending small flames, shifting the burn, and extinguishing other areas.

It all seemed to be going perfectly, and then the wind shifted. It picked up the sparks, fueling them, breathing life into them, until more than the edges were burning. I could see the movements outside becoming more frantic, the controlled burn becoming less controlled. For a few minutes they fought back against the wind and appeared to manage things again—until the wind kicked up once more, and the fire began to spread.

From where I stood in the living room, I could see the fire escalating. I instructed my mom, who was also visiting, to keep an eye on my kids, and I went out to help. The smoke was thick, and the flames were hotter than I had anticipated. I looked to my brother, who asked how much hose we had at the house, and whether I thought it might be able to reach. But that was a fruitless endeavor; the fields were too far from the house for that. My husband's face was a mix of fear and determination as I realized that perhaps the control had left this burn.

We heard sirens from across the field, down on the road below the bluff that houses our property. They seemed to drive past us a few times, circling and then coming back as the sirens whined. *They've never been to our house*, I thought. *How could they even know where we are?* I had images of the fire becoming wild and unruly, swelling and swallowing the wintering fields, reaching up to our log home in the center.

For what seemed like forever, we fought the fire, and the wind, and the racing sirens, until at last a heavy pickup truck ascended our driveway. A neighbor had seen the flames and come to help out. He was smiling. "Got away from ya, huh?" he said to my husband, and I thought I might cry. He took a metal rake from his truck and jumped into the fray.

After a few minutes, they'd regained some degree of control, and not long after, the fire department arrived with their own pickup truck and what looked like backpacks of water and heavy duty super-soakers. At any other time, I might have panicked at the lack of a water truck, hook and ladder, or other typical firefighting equipment, but they entered the fight as though they'd done this a thousand times before—and then the fire was gone. Only white steam smoke remained over the cold, wet field.

We were a little sheepish as we spoke to the firefighters and the kind neighbor. We were, after all, city slickers trying to do the country thing. But the firemen and the neighbor clapped Dave on the back and told him he'd done everything exactly as he ought to have. No one can control the wind, and up there on the bluff, it's even more difficult to gauge. They were impressed he had done as well as this. They told him that even seasoned farmers need help from time to time. "That's our job," they said. They were glad to be of service.

When I consider the fields of me, I think about those times in which I feel as though I am caught in the wildfire out of control. The wind shifts, and I do not know where to go next. Everything around me is on fire, burning and taking down the fields. I think, even then, that I have it under control. I'm inclined to pull away from people, to hunker down, to grab a rake and bat at the flames. My arms are tired and weak now, my lungs burn from the smoke, my eyes are blurry. I cannot see. *Where does my help come from?*

Whether it is the struggle with eating, body image, or exercise, these wildfire moments happen. I cannot control the wind shifts, and something that might feel as though it's been manageable for a long time suddenly burns high with flames leaping. Where eating is concerned, this happens for me in seasons of feasting and in fasting. I aim to keep a balance, but of course, if the winds of stress are changing, I will most likely let that get away from me. With exercise, I let life overwhelm the need to do it well, to do it often, or to do it at all. Sometimes having someone drive up with a super soaker to add some support is the only thing that ensures that wildfire won't take over. Body image, or better yet, loving the body I have right now in any condition it might manifest, is so personal and private. It is this hidden garden that I worry the firefighters cannot even find, but the hidden garden becoming a burning field means that at least someone may notice those smoke signals. Help comes when I need it, if I'm willing to take it.

In those moments, I admit that too often I turn down offers of help. I live with the delusion that maybe I can, with just a little time and a little more elbow grease, pull it all back together. I am thankful for the neighbors with the metal rake, for the firefighters with the super-soakers. Having someone who knows what to do when the field is aflame takes me to a new place of humility. It requires me to admit that I need help and to accept that taking that help is not a sign of weakness, but of strength.

❧❧❧❧❧❧❧

A person who, while having God in mind, honors everyone, will find everyone to be his helper, thanks to the hidden will of God.

—St. Isaac of Syria

A STRONG CORE IN THE BODY helps to keep injury away when life throws physical curves. If you've ever slipped on the ice and caught yourself before you've fallen, you know this feeling. Everything tenses, creating an internal cage that takes the sudden and unexpected change in balance. If we're strong, it shores us up. We remain standing and uninjured, shaken but able to keep going. When the core is weak, that support system is more likely to fail, and we are more likely to fall.

Our core muscles support every action, every twist, every breath—and we do not give them much thought until the ground shifts below us, or we trip or slip, and we find we're off center and meeting the hard concrete. The wind shifts, and the field begins to burn out of control. Having a core that is strong is a kind of protection, like knowing we have neighbors who care or firefighters who know where we live.

The way the muscles of the core in your body work to support movement at every level is very like the role of community in our lives. The elements of any good physical or spiritual practice require some kind of community of support. For some this aspect can be intimidating. Asking for help and accountability is hard. It is humbling to admit that we need help, that we need hands to hold from time to time. We want to be autonomous and self-sustaining—and yet we are creatures of community. We need people. This is what helps us to be strong no matter what comes our way.

I'm convinced that though I know I am an introvert, and though I love the silence, being alone and being self-motivated, it's not enough. I think about that Tom Hanks movie, *Castaway.* The first thing he looks for after food, water, and shelter is companionship. We're made like this, to reach out to one another. We cannot do it alone—no man is an island and all that.

Of the many lies I will encounter as I travel this life road, the idea that I do not need anyone or anything may be the most destructive and self-defeating. As crazy as life becomes, and as noisy as it sounds to this quiet-seeking creature, I still need to reach out to hands that can help hold me fast. When we feel overwhelmed and unprepared to handle the wilderness that surrounds us, it's all right to reach out, to ask for help, to look for guides. This is not a failing.

CHAPTER THIRTEEN

HARVEST

On beginnings and endings

We have within us deeply rooted weaknesses, passions, and defects. This cannot all be cut out with one sharp motion, but patience, persistence, care and attention. The path leading to perfection is long. Pray to God so that he will strengthen you. Patiently accept your falls and, having stood up, immediately run to God, not remaining in that place where you have fallen. Do not despair if you keep falling into your old sins. Many of them are strong because they have received the force of habit. Only with the passage of time and with fervor will they be conquered. Don't let anything deprive you of hope.

—St. Nectarios of Aegina, *Path to Happiness*

The window boxes outside the second-floor window of my maternal grandmother's house were always full of flowers in the spring. She lived a few streets away from us when I was in grade school. The window boxes were always bursting with bloom, but in the winter they were bare and waiting. I would witness my grandmother or my great-grandmother taking up the dying plants, perhaps just after the frost, and clearing the soil of the packed root systems so that it might rest through the frozen winter. The bare and empty window boxes felt hopeful and ready for something new and good.

We did not usually play in that room when we visited her house, but I was entranced by the gauzy ruffled curtains and the huge wall of windows that faced the street, so I would sneak up there. My great-grandmother, Ma, slept in that room when my mother was growing up. After Ma died, my grandmother kept the room immaculate and the flower boxes filled. I would sit by the windows, watching the cars go by, the trees sway outside, the ants crawl around the begonias and petunias in the box in the warm weather, the frost-covered soil in the cold.

Those window boxes remind me of the many times throughout my life when I would admire beauty, yearn for it, but have no idea how to attain it. They remind me of the desperate desire to possess beauty, to see it there blooming and sturdy, and of the crushing disappointment that came when the bloom did not appear. But they remind me, too, of hope. Hope returns to me again and again, with each season, each thaw or heavy snow.

They remind me of this because when my family bought the house a few years later, that room with the window boxes belonged to my sister and me. I tried in vain to keep the boxes filled and blooming. My mother would help me plant new flowers, giving me instructions to water when the weather was dry or to pull weeds when I saw them pop up. I often lost focus or just did not care to listen to the instruction. I wanted the burst of beauty, but I did not want to work that hard for it.

Not long after the window boxes were mine to tend, I was no longer content to sit by the window. I was playing soccer and discovering all the middle-school distractions one could find. I was convinced that my great-grandmother, grandmothers on both sides, and my mother too had secret knowledge, secret gifts, that enabled them to keep growing things growing. In time, I moved on to doing things I was able to master without working outside my comfort zone. I loved the look of the window boxes, but I was not so willing to reach out and discover the best way to get the results. And then life got in the way, and I let it go.

This experience helped build the mythology I developed about my skills and talents—or my lack thereof. It is one story in a lifetime of stories that I realize serve as background noise, whisperings, and nothing more—nothing substantial, nothing true. When I look at that experience—and all the experiences these stories come from—with a good lens, a clean nous, a healthy perspective, what I notice first is the beauty of the process rather than the disappointment in the harvest. The harvest varies from season to season, day to day, but the process, the daily work of the garden, is the real strength here. This is what keeps the avid home gardener engaged season after season. For the gardener who plants because she wants to encounter beauty and help it to thrive in the world around her, the harvest is nice—but it is the process that is healing.

I look to the growing things I have scattered now around my house, my yard, my back deck, and I think about the work it takes to keep it all tended. Growing things need care—like children, like bodies, like relationships. There is no real endpoint to this kind of caring. This kind of tending and nurturing will change, of course, as time wears on, and the needs of that garden, window box, child, or body change. There is planting, and there is harvest—this plays out in new ways each year, and in familiar ways, too. The process of that caretaking is quotidian, moment by moment. Each new moment brings with it a mix of joy and disappointment, and each new moment brings with it renewed hopes and opportunities for growth.

We develop this understanding, this comfort, that comes with time. Those window boxes did not bloom without my care. If I do not plant the flowers I want to see in the spring, they will not surface. I may go through many flats of pansies to get there. I may have to take it all up from time to time, replace the soil and leftover root systems from years of neglect. I will have to get my hands dirty. I will have to persevere despite my bad gardening history and the stories I tell myself about who I am and what I'm capable of. I persevere because of the promise of the harvest, yes, but not just that.

I persevere now, despite all the setbacks and sense of lacking, because of the feel of the earth on my hands, the moments of sun on my shoulders, breaking up the tired root systems to make way for new plantings, fresh air, green leaves, ripe tomatoes. These moments are hopeful. I persevere because of this hope. I am no longer gardening only for the rewards, the successes, the harvest, but for the peace that comes while watering, while planting, while pruning. The hope is for the harvest, but that hope is not deferred until it comes to fruition. It is no longer dependent on a future version of the garden but on the beauty of this moment, this leaf, this twig. It is present in the *now* of what I am doing, how I am moving, eating, or resting.

Whatever I've done in the name of this garden, I can always return to this hope—hope for health, hope for peace, and perhaps, at last, a strong relationship with this body. I hear the words of St. Nectarios echo then, knowing that only with the passage of time and with fervor will my fears and doubts be overcome. I will not let anything deprive me of that hope.

I hope for the chance to look back upon my seasons and see the good that came from each. I hope for a time when I can look in the mirror and know deep within myself, say without any hesitation, that this body is flourishing and fecund, strong and capable, beautiful and true—and that it is good. This body is a garden, and I'm grateful for it—regardless of the season, the harvest, the condition, I am grateful.

The body is a garden.

Angela Doll Carlson is a poet, fiction writer, and essayist whose work has appeared in publications such as *St. Katherine Review, Rock & Sling Journal, Ruminate Magazine, Ink & Letters, Whale Road Review, Elephant Journal, Relief Journal,* and *Art House America.* Her memoir, *Nearly Orthodox: On Being a Modern Woman in an Ancient Tradition,* was published by Ancient Faith Publishing in 2014.

You can also find her writing online at NearlyOrthodox.com, MrsMetaphor.com, and DoxaSoma.com and hear her podcast, *The Wilderness Journal,* on AncientFaith.com.

Angela currently lives in Chicago, Illinois, with her husband, David, and her four outrageously spirited yet remarkably likable children.

ADDITIONAL READING
(ALPHABETICAL BY AUTHOR)

The Secret Garden
Frances Hodgson Burnett
Signet; Reissue edition (July 1, 2003)

Endless Life: Poems of the Mystics
Scott Cairns
Paraclete Press (February 1, 2014)

The Art of Prayer: An Orthodox Anthology
Igumen Chariton
Farrar, Straus and Giroux; Revised edition (July 31, 1997)

A Book of Hours
Patricia Colling Egan
Conciliar Press/Ancient Faith Publishing, 2010

Inheriting Paradise: Meditations on Gardening
Vigen Guroian
Wm. B. Eerdmans Publishing Co. (April 14, 1999)

The Fragrance of God
Vigen Guroian
Wm. B. Eerdmans (2007)

The Human Body: Ascesis and Exercise
Met. Hierotheos of Nafpaktos
Birth of Theotokos Monastery Pelagia (2004)

The Mystical Theology of the Eastern Church
Vladimir Lossky
St. Vladimir's Seminary Press (March 1997)

The Wilderness of God
Andrew Louth
Abingdon Press (March 1997)

**Food, Faith, and Fasting: A Sacred Journey
to Better Health**
Rita Madden
Ancient Faith Publishing, 2015

An Inner Step Toward God
Fr. Alexander Men
Paraclete Press (March 1, 2014)

**The Teaching of the Holy Fathers on the Body
(pamphlet)**
Nikodemos Orthodox Publication Society (1997)

The Scent of Holiness
Constantina Palmer
Conciliar Press/Ancient Faith Publishing, 2012

**The Philokalia: The Complete Text (Vol. 1);
Compiled by St. Nikodemos of the Holy Mountain and
St. Markarios of Corinth**
G.E.H. Palmer, Philip Sherrard, Kallistos Ware
Ttranslators)
Farrar, Straus and Giroux (January 1, 1983)

Theology of the Body in Simple Language
Pope John Paul II (Author), Philokalia Books (Adapter)
CreateSpace Independent Publishing Platform (April 11, 2009)

Encounters with Silence
Karl Rahner
St. Augustine's Press (June 30, 1999)

John Cassian: Conferences
Boniface Ramsey (Translator)
Paulist Press (November 1, 1997)

For the Life of the World: Sacraments and Orthodoxy
Alexander Schmemann
St. Vladimir's Seminary Press (1973)

Adventure of Ascent: Field Notes from a Lifelong Journey
Luci Shaw
IVP Books (2014)

Thumbprint in the Clay: Divine Marks of Beauty, Order and Grace
Luci Shaw
IVP Books (March 16, 2016)

Straight Out of View
Joyce Sutphen
Holy Cow! Press (2001)

Intuitive Eating
Evelyn Tribole and Elyse Resch
St. Martin's Griffin; 3rd edition (August 7, 2012)

The Sayings of the Desert Fathers: The Alphabetical Collection
Benedicta Ward (Translator, Foreword), Metropolitan Anthony (Preface)
Liturgical Press; Revised edition (1984)

Bread and Water, Wine and Oil
Archimandrite Meletios Webber
Conciliar Press/Ancient Faith Publishing, 2007

Ancient Faith Publishing hopes you have enjoyed and benefited from this book. The proceeds from the sales of our books only partially cover the costs of operating our non-profit ministry—which includes both the work of **Ancient Faith Publishing** and the work of **Ancient Faith Radio**. Your financial support makes it possible to continue this ministry both in print and online. Donations are tax-deductible and can be made at www.ancientfaith.com.

To request a catalog of other publications,
please call us at (800) 967-7377 or (219) 728-2216
or log onto our website: **store.ancientfaith.com**

Bringing you Orthodox Christian music, readings,
prayers, teaching, and podcasts 24 hours a day since 2004
at **www.ancientfaith.com**